ONE BY ONE
Daisaku Ikeda

ONE BY ONE

Daisaku Ikeda

DUNHILL PUBLISHING

One by One
By Daisaku Ikeda

Published by:
Dunhill Publishing
18340 Sonoma Highway
Sonoma, CA 95476
(707) 939-9212

Copyright © 2005 Soka Gakkai
First Edition
Printed in the United States of America

Cover Photo © 2005 Estate of Pablo Picasso / Artists Rights Society (ARS), New York

---

Publisher's Cataloging-in-Publication
(Provided by Quality Books, Inc.)

    Ikeda, Daisaku
       One by One / Daisaku Ikeda.
       p. cm.
       ISBN 1-931501-01-7
       Includes bibiographical references.
       LCCN 2004105747

     1. Peace. 2. Peace-building. 3. Violence.
    4. Security, International. I. Title.

    JZ5538.I34 2004   303.6'6
                      QBI04-700290

TABLE OF CONTENTS

INTRODUCTION

It is a rare pleasure for me to present this introduction of a very special work by a very special person. This selection of essays by Daisaku Ikeda has brought out the brilliant mind and all-embracing compassion of a person for whom I have profound respect and deep friendship. His insight into the human mind and emotions has found a remarkable expression in this simple and at the same time absolutely absorbing writing style. His power of analyzing an apparently not-so-significant incident or individual and finding something very profound is fascinating. I enjoyed reading each one of the essays that presents to the reader a shining example of human spirit. The breadth of his vision, and the conviction with which he assures us that a bright future is possible individually and collectively, are deeply inspiring, particularly at a time when the need for such a message of hope and belief in humanity's inherent strength is keenly felt.

Mr. Ikeda's life has been enriched by his constant quest for the essence of human spirit and for humanity's nirvana. His meetings with people from various walks of life assume special significance through his dialogues about the future of humanity against the backdrop of the horrible tragedies of the twentieth century. Having witnessed and experienced the worst, the saddest losses that life can bring—the loss of loved ones in war, the pain of separation and, worst of all, of not knowing the fate of those precious people—these individuals show us that life does continue, that the light of hope can be found in the very darkest corners. Mr. Ikeda has brought out their most valued feelings and thoughts in a wonderfully genuine style of writing.

When we read these real-life examples of the strength of the human mind and spirit, we too can find the will to remain undaunted in our own personal or working lives in the face of heavy odds. As in his own life Mr. Ikeda has always refused to kowtow to hatred, injustice and human tyranny, the persons in these essays representing all corners of our world emerge as the epitome of humanity's eternal struggle to establish a just and humane society.

Mr. Ikeda's collection of essays bears an eloquent testimony to his own life's mission of bringing out the goodness of humanity by championing dialogue that promotes understanding and respect. He has devoted his life to a cause which we share—that of building a culture of peace. A world in which every individual is treasured not in spite of, but because of his or her uniqueness and difference. A world in which we make the effort to understand the sufferings and the hopes of others and to reach out to them across every divide with faith in our common humanity and the preciousness of life. He has dedicated himself to help create such a world and in this endeavor he has come across people who have enriched his life and contributed to his mission. Their stories do come alive in the compassionate writings of Mr. Ikeda.

Through the pages that follow you will meet many extraordinary people. Some of them are already known to you. You will also learn about Mr. Ikeda's own experiences of growing up in wartime Japan and how they shaped his desire to contribute to building a peaceful world, one step at a time. I hope, like me, you will be encouraged to believe that every one of us does matter, that our choices and our actions do shape our future.

ANWARUL CHOWDHURY
Under-Secretary-General
United Nations

PROLOGUE

I have a photograph that stirs the fondest of memories. It is a picture in which I am holding the arm of British historian Arnold J. Toynbee as we walk together through the bustling streets of London. I believe it was taken either before or after we had shared a stimulating discussion over lunch at a local restaurant. Though frail with age and suffering from heart problems, the eminent scholar continued our dialogue as we made our way. I felt his words were of great significance—to me now and for the future.

In the fall of 1969 I had received a letter from Dr. Toynbee. During a visit to Japan in 1967 he had heard a great deal about the lay Buddhist association, Soka Gakkai, of which I had assumed leadership seven years earlier, succeeding my mentor, Josei Toda, as president.

"It is my pleasure, therefore," he wrote, "to extend to you my personal invitation to visit me in Britain in order to have with you a fruitful exchange of views on a number of fundamental problems of our time which deeply concern us all…"

Thus it was that in May 1972, I found myself standing in front of Dr. Toynbee's residence in London's Oakwood Court, a deep, ocher-colored building. Our small party, consisting of myself, my wife and a trio of interpreters—one to interpret from English to Japanese, one from Japanese to English, and the third to record our conversations on tape—went up in an old-fashioned elevator to the fifth floor apartment where the Toynbees lived. We were greeted by the tall white-haired professor, his eyes shining behind glasses, and his wife, Veronica. Over the course of the next few days we shared views with great intentness from morning till early evening.

Our dialogue covered a wide range of themes, from perspectives on life, the future of global civilization, environmental destruction, war and international affairs, to health and welfare and the problems involved in globalization. The topics of our discussion seemed to expand infinitely and our dialogue proceeded at such a rapid pace that the interpreters were often overwhelmed.

Once, during our dialogue, I asked Dr. Toynbee what the saddest experience in his life was. His warm and friendly expression immediately stiffened, as if he were trying to mask a profound sorrow, and for a moment I regretted having posed the question. "That would be when one of my sons chose to commit suicide in the next room." Sunk deep into the sofa, his hands clasped, Dr. Toynbee was as motionless as a statue.

I realized then that the study where Dr. Toynbee worked was also a place where, enduring the cruel trials of fate, he pondered the questions of life and death.

What is human existence? What gives life its dignity? Dr. Toynbee sought out people with whom he could discuss these fundamental issues. He always probed the essential nature of events.

His lifework *A Study of History* was actually the study of humanity. He cultivated a sympathy for those who had been ignored and oppressed throughout history. For him, to attach importance only to dominant cultures was to close one's eyes to half of human history. Dr. Toynbee respectfully studied ancient civilizations as well as contemporary societies that had been overshadowed by the modern West. His humanistic perspective of history inevitably led to the study of religion, in order to explore the relationship between human beings and the universe. At the end of his intellectual quest, he concluded that people's own transformation, namely the conquest of selfishness and the practice of love, is what will save humanity from ruin.

When I asked Dr. Toynbee what he wished to do the most, he responded, "It would be what we are doing right here in this room. In other words, our dialogue taking place here signifies the effort to unite humanity as one large family."

With a hearing aid and chronic heart ailments, he carried out our long hours of dialogue with all his might. I was struck by his unswerving determination to set down and leave behind his thoughts.

What distinguishes first-class individuals from others? In my view, it is essentially the fact that they focus their gaze on posterity, and base their thoughts and action on the welfare of future generations. Those who do so have a vision. They are not swayed by short-term phenomena of the present. Dr. Toynbee was extraordinary in that sense.

If the leaders of our society pondered, even for a single moment, what the world will be like after their death, and considered what should be done now based on that perspective, the world would change dramatically from that day onward.

The common conclusion that Dr. Toynbee and I arrived at through our dialogue is that life transcends all things and that its sanctity is the point from which all things arise and to which all things must return.

In 1973 he again invited me to come to London so that we could continue our discussion face-to-face.

In all, our dialogue lasted for a total of nearly 40 hours. When Dr. Toynbee suggested that we publish the dialogue, I originally declined the idea, believing my lack of education made me an unworthy partner to one of the world's most renowned historians. I was eventually convinced by his strong urge to leave it for posterity.

A year later, Dr. Toynbee fell ill. He passed away in the following autumn at the age of 86. To date, our dialogue *Choose Life* has been published in over 20 languages. I have often been surprised by unexpected comments and impressions on the book from people I've met in various countries.

On the last day of our dialogue, as we were about to part upon completing our discussion, Dr. Toynbee handed one of the interpreters a list of the world's leading intellects that he recommended I seek out. The interpreter later conveyed what I took as Dr. Toynbee's parting message to me. The gist of it was that while our talks had come to a conclusion, he expected me to engage in similar discussions with others at every possible opportunity.

Our exchange took place in the midst of the Cold War. The United States and the Soviet Union led hostile opposing blocs, and there was a climate of enmity between the Soviet Union and China. After my dialogue with Dr. Toynbee, I proceeded to visit all three nations in succession.

In every country, I found people who shared a common humanity and a deep desire for peace. I became convinced that dialogue was the means to melt the frigid walls of mistrust dividing us. That conviction remains unchanged to this day.

Since that time, I have continued to seek out and meet with leading thinkers and proponents of change from various backgrounds and cultures. Each of these people has brought something of unique value to the world, often persevering through tremendous struggles and in the face of huge obstacles. In writing about them, my hope has been to share with others the wisdom and the courage that each has demonstrated through their often extraordinary lives.

I would be especially happy if these essays were to serve as a source of hope and inspiration to young people, who are the architects and inheritors of the future. As these individuals I have been fortunate to encounter have demonstrated, every single one of us can make a difference and can in fact change the world.

Daisaku Ikeda
September 2004

Arnold Toynbee

Another Way of Seeing Things

ARNOLD TOYNBEE (1889–1975), UNITED KINGDOM
Once referred to as "an international sage" by TIME magazine, historian Arnold Toynbee received wide recognition for his ten-volume A Study of History, acknowledged as one of the great achievements of modern scholarship. In it Toynbee examined the rise and fall of civilizations, determined by their ability to respond to challenges. He gave particular stress to the influence of religion in this process. Toynbee served in the British Foreign Office, as Research Professor of International History at the University of London and Director of Studies at the Royal Institute of International Affairs.

Arnold Toynbee

Another Way of Seeing Things

Every country offers a different perspective. For example, in Japan, apartments with a western exposure, because they are hot in the afternoon, are usually cheaper. But in sun-starved northern Europe such an apartment will command a premium.

In some cultures it is considered rude to look a person directly in the eye when addressing them, while in others it is rude not to. In Japan it is perfectly acceptable to hold one's rice bowl as one eats. In Korea this is considered vulgar.

Whereas in some countries it is polite to keep a certain distance when talking to someone, in Arab countries there is a tradition that values savoring the fragrance of a friend's breath. Thus an attempt to observe a polite distance could give offense as a sign of cold aloofness.

Attitudes toward the nation and state also differ. There are people who are ready to give their lives for their beloved homeland. There are also those who think of the state simply as a provider of social services and would be happy to live in any country that provides such services well.

Before we debate the respective merits of different views and values, I think it is important that we first recognize that differences do exist. As the world continues to grow smaller, our ability to understand people of other cultures becomes more and more crucial.

In New York City several years ago I understand there was a conflict between the Korean and Haitian communities in which cultural differences played an important role. When Haitians speak to each other, they frequently reach out and touch the other person's hand or shoulder as an expression of intimacy and warmth. But in most East Asian cultures such gestures are generally not welcomed. The discomfort of the Koreans with such personal contact was perceived by the Haitians as a sign of racial discrimination.

The Korean grocers also prided themselves on arranging their wares neatly on the shelves, and didn't want them handled needlessly. On the other hand, for Haitians, it is customary to pick something up and discuss its value at length before settling on a price.

The bad feelings and friction arising from such cultural misperceptions built up between the two communities to the point that a boycott against Korean-owned grocery stores was initiated.

Where deep bonds of trust have been established, we can experience cultural differences as the fresh discovery of other ways of looking at the world. We can further enhance our sense of mutual respect. All too often, however, such differences end up being the cause of misunderstanding and conflict.

And nothing is more damaging than acts that force one's own culture and values on others.

I am aware of a family in Japan in which the father is from an Islamic country. The mother is Japanese, and the child attends a Japanese school. Whenever the school lunch contained pork, the consumption of which is prohibited in Islam, the parents would request that their child be allowed to bring a bag lunch from home. But the school refused, saying that eating what everyone else eats is part of the pupils' education. The child ended up doing without lunch on those days.

An old saying has it, "When in Rome, do as the Romans do." If you wish to follow local customs yourself, that is fine. But you cannot force others to do so. Some Japanese, though aware that followers of Islam may not drink liquor, try to impose it on them, saying, "This is Japan, so drink up!" or "Unless we drink together, we can't really open up."

There is a tendency in Japan toward the kind of collectivism that values rigid conformity in all things. Some non-Japanese comment that the most unpleasant thing about living in Japan is being told that "that's how everyone is" or "that's what everyone does" with the implication that what's right for the majority is right for everyone.

We need to make the effort to find out what the other person is really thinking. But we are hampered by our failure to recognize our own arrogance, the arrogance that keeps us from truly hearing the views and opinions of others.

We live in an age of multicultural encounter. How can we assure that those encounters will not be dissonant clashes but can resound as the joyous harmony of different voices?

DEVELOPING A GLOBAL PERSPECTIVE

I have long felt that Turkey, as a country pivotally linking East and West, North and South, has a unique role to play in fostering the harmony of humankind.

Turkey embraces both Asia and Europe. In 1992, on my first visit to Turkey in 30 years, I found myself in Istanbul gazing at the Bosporus Strait. The land on the west side of the narrow strait was Europe; that on the east, Asia. Travelers from the West encounter the cultural richness of the East, and those from the East can encounter the West, champion of modernization. To both, the world begins to show a new and different face.

To the north lie Russia and the Slavic world; to the south, the Mediterranean and Africa.

Turkey is the land of the poet Homer's birth. It was crossed by the conquering Alexander the Great. Classical Greek civilization once flourished here. During the Byzantine Empire, it was a leading center of the Christian world. And later, under the Ottoman Turks, it was the heart of Islamic civilization.

Mirroring its kaleidoscopic history, Turkey today is a place of immense human diversity. In the towns and cities one can see people with Arab and Mongolian features, people with faces reminiscent of Greek statues, Russian faces, Eastern European faces...

It is as if the land of Turkey is trying to encompass all humanity and make it one, calling out: "West, you may be East in my embrace! East, you may be West in my home!"

For the historian Dr. Arnold Toynbee (1889–1975), Turkey had a particular significance, as it was events in Turkey that prompted him to become a pioneer in looking beyond the Eurocentric view of history. During our conversations in his London apartment, he told me that he had once been forced to quit his post at London University because he had "angered people prejudiced against Turks" with his straightforward reporting of events in Turkey.

Toynbee visited Turkey in 1921, when he was about 32 years old. He had gone to observe the Greco-Turkish War that had been raging for two years. He first observed conditions from the Greek side, then from the Turkish. For Toynbee, guided as he was by Saint Augustine's injunction *"Audi alteram partem"* (Hear the other side), this was absolutely crucial. And he placed particular importance on listening to the side that was "the more in danger of not being given a fair hearing":

If one was to see straight, one must also see things from the mute party's point of view...

In the present conflict and controversy between Greeks and Turks, the Greeks were the vocal party once again. The Greeks had the ear of the West, and the West was in the ascendant in the world. I was familiar with the Greeks' case; I felt that it could take care of itself; the Turks' case was the one that I must take pains to understand.

Toynbee traveled to a town where Turkish civilians had been massacred. He witnessed the suffering of Turkish refugees, and was outraged that these atrocities went completely unreported in the West. Writing down the facts exactly as he had seen them, he wired these to the *Manchester Guardian*, a leading British newspaper. The editor of the paper courageously published the full texts of Toynbee's reports.

Why "courageously"?

For centuries the Turks had been portrayed in the West as uncivilized savages. To make matters worse, the horrors of the 1915 Armenian Massacre[1] carried out by the Ottoman Turks were still fresh in people's memories. And indeed, when the articles appeared, the newspaper was besieged by a storm of criticism. People attacked it for shamelessly publishing articles sympathetic to the "unspeakable Turk." But the paper's admirable stance of refusing to bend to what Toynbee saw as prejudice against Muslims shines to this day.

At the other end of the spectrum, the article made a deep impression on the Turks. They were astonished that a young Englishman had visited a Turkish refugee camp, that he had impartially recorded what he had seen, and that a British newspaper had actually published it. It was the first time their side of the story had been conveyed to the world. Years later Toynbee animatedly recounted how Turkish people gathered around the newspaper, their faces flushed with excitement as they read his article.

MULTIPLE PERSPECTIVES

Relying only on information from the West—viewing things always from the Western perspective—does not provide a true picture of the world. There is an African view of the world, a world seen from the Middle East, from Latin America, through the eyes of various ethnic minorities. There is more to international society than just the West.

---

[1] It is estimated that as many as 1.5 million Armenians were killed in what is considered the first genocide of the 20th century. Arnold Toynbee exhaustively researched these atrocities, assisting with the preparation of a 700-page account of the subject for the British Government.

On his homeward journey by train from Istanbul, Toynbee began to outline what would become his lifework, *A Study of History*. Based on those notes, he later developed the groundbreaking historical theory—written from a global perspective—that was his great gift to humankind.

Shortly after his return to Britain, Toynbee was forced to resign from his post at London University over what was seen as his support for the Turks. He told me that for the next 33 years, he made his living writing reports on international issues for the Royal Institute of International Affairs, an independent research organization.

The young Toynbee knew it was wrong to stereotype and thus dehumanize people as the Turks had been. It was necessary to get to know individual Turks. He put this conviction into practice, learning Turkish and making friends with Turkish people. "When one becomes personally acquainted with a fellow human being, of whatever religion, nationality, or race, one cannot fail to recognize that he is human like oneself…"

THE TYRANNY OF IMAGES

Has the danger of stereotyping people lessened since the days of Dr. Toynbee's youth? I don't believe so. In fact, what I call the "tyranny of images"—that is, the propagation of stereotypes and ready-made images—may have even increased.

For example, I know of a Japanese journalist who had heard that despite Scandinavian countries' advanced social welfare policies, many of the elderly suffered from isolation and there was a high suicide rate among them. When he visited Sweden, he offended people by asking what park he could visit to photograph lonely old people sitting on benches.

Much of the information that floods our world has been selected and tailored to fit preconceived notions and stereotypes.

In the extremity of wartime, repeatedly airing scenes of "our side" coming under attack will incite and outrage the populace. In contrast, scenes of the hellish misery inflicted on the citizens of the other country will rarely be broadcast.

The growth and development of various media can actually increase the danger of proliferating stereotypes and ready-made images. We are all exposed to these risks.

It is vital that we each ask ourselves some important questions. For example: Do I accept without question the images provided to me? Do I believe unconfirmed reports without first examining them? Have I unwittingly allowed myself to become prejudiced? Do I really have a grasp of the facts of the matter? Have I confirmed things for myself? Have I gone to the scene? Have I met the people involved? Have I listened to what they have to say? Am I being swayed by malicious rumors?

I believe that this kind of "inner dialogue" is crucial. This is because people who are aware that they may harbor unconscious prejudices can converse with people of other cultures more easily than those who are convinced that they have no prejudices.

When we stop looking at ourselves, when we no longer question ourselves, we become self-righteous and dogmatic. Our discourse becomes a one-way street: We cannot hear others, and real dialogue becomes impossible.

The kind of dialogue that can create peace with others must start with an open and earnest "inner dialogue."

CITIZENS OF EARTH

If we think about it, people are not born Turks or Americans. They are not born Palestinians or Jews. These are merely labels.

Each of us is born as a precious entity of life, as a human being. Our mothers didn't give birth to us thinking, "I'm giving birth to a Japanese" or "I'm giving birth to an Arab." Their only thought was "May this new life be healthy and grow!"

In any country, a rose is a rose, a violet is a violet, people are people—though they may be called by different names.

Perhaps the clouds and winds high above the blue waters of the Bosporus are whispering among themselves as they gaze down upon humanity: "Wake up! From up here, it is clear that the world is one. You are all citizens of Earth. There is no such thing as Americans, no such thing as Iraqis. There is only this boy, this life, called Bob, who happens to live in America; there is only this boy, this life, Mohammed, who happens to live in Iraq. Both are children of Earth. And yet they are divided by the names of their countries and taught to hate each other! Wake up from this foolishness, this arrogance, this cruel habit of passing hatred and resentment on to the next generation."

We need to awaken to a common consciousness of being all inhabitants of Earth. This consciousness is not to be found in some distant place. It will not be found on a computer screen. It lies in our hearts, in our ability to share the pain of our fellow human beings. It is the spirit that says: "As long as you are suffering, whoever you are and whatever your suffering may be, I suffer also."

Jose Abueva

Refusing to Hate

JOSE V. ABUEVA (1928–), THE PHILIPPINES

Dr. Abueva was president of the University of the Philippines from 1987 to 1992 where he is professor emeritus of political science and public administration. In 2001, he became founding president of Kalayaan College which encourages its students to pursue truth and freedom and contribute to social transformation. Formerly secretary and director of planning and evaluation at the United Nations University in Tokyo, Dr. Abueva has also taught at the City University of New York and Yale University.

JOSE ABUEVA

Refusing to Hate

⟿

It was 1944. The sixteen-year-old-boy dragged the oars through the water again and the small boat moved slowly against the shoreline. He was searching for his parents who had been taken prisoner by Japanese soldiers occupying the Philippines. The boy's father, Teodoro Abueva, had refused to cooperate with the invaders of his homeland, becoming a member of the Bohol Provincial Board in the anti-Japanese resistance government. The boy's mother, Nena Veloso Abueva, was head of the Bohol Women's Auxiliary Service in the resistance. Teodoro and Nena had three daughters and four sons; the boy in the boat was their second son, Jose.

Thus begin some of the recollections that Dr. Jose Abueva, former president of the University of the Philippines, kindly wrote down for me under the title "Our Family Story of War and Peace, Love and Remembrance." He continues…

The Japanese military had hunted Teodoro for a long time. On one occasion, they captured his sons Jose and Billy as well as his mother. But they let Jose go and told him to tell Teodoro that if he wanted to see the others again, he must surrender to the Japanese.

Several days later, Billy came staggering back home, groaning in pain. He was almost unrecognizable. His face was swollen, his front teeth knocked out, and his body bruised and battered. The implied threat to Teodoro from the Japanese military was clear: "If you continue to resist, we will also torture and kill your mother." But Billy carried a secret message to Teodoro from her: "Do not surrender, no matter what happens to me. I am old. You have a wife and seven children to live for."

A year later, after hiding in the mountains with the rest of the guerrilla forces, the Abueva family—except for Jose and Billy who were living with others—were captured. The Japanese military separated husband and wife and tortured them. The children were forced to listen to their parents' agonized screams. Then the soldiers took Teodoro and Nena away, freeing the children. Billy looked after his brothers and sisters while Jose, together with a cousin, set out in a boat in search of his parents.

TRAGIC CLIMB

It was to be a sad journey. Jose landed at the town where the family had been taken. News of the American recapture of the Philippines was spreading, and there was not a Japanese soldier to be seen. Praying that by some miracle his parents might still be alive, Jose searched for a clue to their whereabouts. He heard rumors of people who had been killed and hurled down a cliff, and was advised to start his search there. As Jose came closer to the cliff, he heard more stories of resistance members being executed on a nearby hillside and set off in that direction. But still he refused to believe his parents were dead. He climbed the hill. The sun shone down fiercely from a cloudless sky. He walked into a clearing with some bushes beyond it. Suddenly, an acrid smell hit his nostrils as he came upon an executioner's handiwork. He saw a soiled white shirt with blue stripes and immediately recognized it as his father's. Then he saw a piece of his mother's brown dress. He also found fragments of rosaries and belts that he recognized as having belonged to them.

Despite the horror of the experience, Jose didn't cry. He was so emotionally and physically drained, tears would not come. When he noticed his surroundings, he was looking to the shining sea stretching toward

Mindanao. Thoughts of what had happened to his parents flooded his mind. They were martyrs who had fought for their love of freedom and their love for their country. For that they had been tortured and killed. This hill was where their lives had ended in such a cruel sacrifice. He heard that the bodies had been left there for more than a week, exposed to the elements and wild animals.

Jose gathered his parents' remains and got back in the boat. The sea of his homeland was almost blindingly beautiful. The Allied forces under General MacArthur had already landed on the Filipino island of Leyte on October 20. Jose's parents had been killed on October 23. For them, the liberation of the Philippines had come just moments too late.

The surviving seven children decided their parents' tomb should be in a garden next to the town's elementary school. Friends and relatives gathered and a Mass was said in their honor. Dr. Abueva writes, "Looking at the big crowd from the veranda, I was one with our grieving family. I finally broke down and cried my heart out. ...Although this story happened half a century ago, it is indelibly etched in my mind. I will never be able to forget." How many others will face the demonic cruelty and madness of war—memories that can never be erased?

In sharing his recollections, Dr. Abueva also observed: "For many years Japanese leaders stubbornly refused to admit—and apologize for—the grievous wrongs they committed in the countries they invaded in World War II. Japanese history textbooks have purposely concealed the truth, or justified the wrongs. Fellow Asians," he continued, "were outraged by the insensitivity and dishonesty of the Japanese. How could they gloss over the sordid truth that so many had witnessed and endured, recorded and remembered?"

TURNING POINT

After the war, the orphaned Abueva children pulled together to support each other as they struggled to continue their education. The siblings would go on to contribute to society in such fields as the arts and education. Jose Abueva studied at the University of the Philippines and then the University of Michigan before eventually returning to become a professor at his *alma mater*.

During his distinguished career in education and development, he has served in posts around the world, including Nepal, Thailand, Lebanon, the United States and Japan. His fond memories of his loving parents have sustained him wherever he has gone, and his determination to work for peace is still motivated by his wish to honor them. All that he has achieved, he says, started with his climb up that hill on that fateful day. He has been utterly devoted to peace, determined to keep others from experiencing the kind of tragedy that he did.

When Dr. Abueva spoke at Tokyo's Soka University in April 1990, he expressed concern about any moves that Japan might make toward rearmament. But he showed no trace of personal bitterness: "My parents were killed by Japanese soldiers. But none of us seven children bears any hatred toward Japan. I like the Japanese. And I believe the people of Japan and the Philippines share the same love of peace."

I was amazed: even through extreme suffering, he has maintained his noble beliefs. Truly he is a greathearted person. How has he been able to overcome the urge, so understandable in his case, to bitterness and hate? He himself wonders how it has been possible to forgive, and credits his parents' religiosity and their "message of love and forgiveness in the midst of suffering and death."

"The great irony of my life," he remarks, "was my recruitment to serve at the headquarters of the United Nations University in Tokyo." For a total of almost eight years, Dr. Abueva and his family lived in Japan, the land of their former enemies.

During their first year in Tokyo, his children often asked: Why did the Japanese kill our grandparents? Dr. Abueva could only explain that his parents had resisted Japanese invaders from love of their country and had paid for that love with their lives.

At the United Nations University (UNU) Dr. Abeuva worked with a team of talented and dedicated scholars from throughout the world to advance UNU's mission of coordinating research on such global issues as eliminating hunger, managing natural resources and promoting social development. Throughout their stay in Japan, Dr. Abueva and his family made a conscious effort to make friends and be ambassadors of goodwill, learning the Japanese language and culture. "By living, learning and working in Japan, by fate or accident, we'd like to feel that we helped to achieve on a limited scale a reconciliation between Filipinos and Japanese."

FOSTERING LEADERS FOR PEACE

Returning to the Philippines, Dr. Abueva helped Corazon Aquino in peace talks between the government and the MNLF separatist guerrillas in the south of the country. In 1987, he was elected president of the University of the Philippines.

"Throughout history there have been many leaders of war," he declared with great passion, "but there have been few leaders of peace. I am determined to help change this."

The University of the Philippines is the country's top school, and its graduates are destined to become leaders in all fields of Philippine society. But Dr. Abueva was concerned that the students also be aware of their duty to society, that they have the willingness and enthusiasm to lead the way in finding solutions to the problems that confront their country. It is his firm belief that a university must above all deepen students' qualities as leaders in the service of their people and country.

Dr. Abueva told me that on becoming university president what had saddened him most was the decline in enrollment of students from poorer families. To rectify the situation, he instituted a policy by which students of wealthy families paid higher tuition fees to subsidize those of poor students.

As president, he put special emphasis on the creation of a "House of Peace" for international exchange. I am very proud that exchange students from Soka University have studied at the University of the Philippines and

I am deeply grateful for Dr. Abueva's kindness to them, even inviting them to his home. He believes that building deeper relations between peoples is even more important than focusing on relations between governments. In particular, he sees youth and cultural exchanges as vital currents in the great flowing river of peace that he is determined to create.

HOUSE OF PEACE

In May 1993 Dr. Abueva invited me to the official opening of the Balay Kalinaw or House of Peace at the University of the Philippines. He also named the building the Ikeda Hall, saying that he hoped it would be a symbol of friendship between the Philippines and Japan. In my remarks on that occasion, I talked about my mentor Josei Toda, second president of the Soka Gakkai, who also stood up against Japanese militarism and who was imprisoned for two years as a result. He was deeply convinced that Japan could only be considered a nation of peace to the extent that it is trusted by its Asian neighbors.

I also declared my determination to devote my life, as an individual Japanese citizen, to the people of Asia. Without mutual understanding, we can achieve nothing.

At that time I quoted the following lines of poetry which were composed by the great Filipino poet and national hero Jose Rizal, who was executed in 1896 before he saw his dream of independence for his homeland realized:

> I die without seeing the dawn
> Brighten over my native land!
> You, who have it to see, welcome it—
> And forget not those
> Who have fallen during the night!

Dr. Abueva's parents were among those who fell in the night, without seeing the dawn of peace. I shared my belief that the same cry must have issued from his parents' lives as they entrusted him with his mission.

I saw Dr. Abueva remove his glasses. As he dabbed at the tears that filled his eyes, I felt I caught a glimpse of a half century of his family's life.

In response to my speech, Dr. Abueva rose from his seat and quoted from a poem of his own:

> *We want an end to killing and maiming*
> *caused by greed or creed, class or tribe*
> *because the poor are weak and the strong are unjust.*

His voice rang through the House of Peace, and it seemed to reach all the way to that hill he climbed so many years ago.

NELSON MANDELA

Lion of Freedom

NELSON MANDELA (1918–), SOUTH AFRICA

A lawyer by training, Mandela became a central figure in the African National Congress (ANC), leading resistance to South Africa's apartheid system. In 1964 he was sentenced to life imprisonment, becoming an international symbol of oppressed peoples. In 1990, he was released and represented the ANC in negotiations that led to the country's first democratic elections in 1994. As South Africa's first black president (1994–99) Mandela presided over the transition from minority rule and apartheid, winning international respect for his promotion of reconciliation.

NELSON MANDELA

Lion of Freedom

⸺⸱⸺

There is something very special about Nelson Mandela's smile. It is honest and pure, full of gentle composure. There isn't a single line on his face that would suggest anything cold or harsh. And yet it embodies the convictions and strength of character of a man who has led his people to freedom. It is a smile like purest gold, from which all impurities have been burned and driven in the furnace of great suffering.

He was brimming with confidence when we met in Tokyo on a July afternoon in 1995. It was our second meeting, some five years after the first, and also a little over a year since he had been elected president of South Africa. He seemed to have grown stronger and wiser with the passage of time, as a mighty, deep-rooted tree continues its ceaseless growth. His bearing offered living proof of the saying that high positions, which make small people smaller, make great people greater.

The "dangerous criminal" who had been imprisoned for 27 years for high treason had emerged from that prison to become president of his country. He symbolized the fact that justice, which had been locked away for so many decades, had finally begun to reign again in South Africa.

Throughout our conversation, his humor and smile never waned. Even in prison, he was a master of the art of using humor to keep up the morale of his comrades.

"MANDELA UNIVERSITY"

The intensity and scale of his struggle stagger the imagination. His imprisonment dragged on for twenty-seven-and-a-half years, more than ten thousand days. As he himself has said, "South Africa's prisons were intended to cripple us so that we should never again have the strength and courage to pursue our ideals."

Uniforms at Robben Island, South Africa's maximum security prison for political prisoners, were deliberately chosen to rob the prisoners of their dignity. Some prisoners were given oversize, baggy clothing, while others had to wear clothes so small that adult men were made to look like children. The food was not fit for human consumption and the bedding—mere paper-thin blankets—provided scant protection against the bitter cold of winter. The prisoners were awakened before dawn to start a long day of forced labor, which sometimes included being made to build their own cells. Back in his solitary cell, barely three paces from wall to wall, time passed agonizingly slowly, and, he recalls, "an hour seemed like a year."

For 13 years Mandela was forced to quarry limestone. Led to the quarry in chains, he had to extract lime from the hard cliffs beneath a burning sun. The stone, however, remained impervious to repeated blows of the pick, the shock of which made his hands go numb. Even then, the guards, one of whom had a Nazi swastika tattooed on his wrist, continued to harangue him to work harder. Over time, the dust from the limestone damaged his eyes.

The prison regulations were vicious and humiliating. To make matters worse, the rules were subject to the whim of the guards, offering the prisoners no hope of fair treatment.

Even under these hellish conditions, Mandela managed to study and encouraged the other prisoners to share their knowledge with each other and to debate their ideas. Lectures were arranged in secrecy and the prison came to be known as "Mandela University."

Mandela never relented in his efforts to change mistaken views and create allies among those around him. Eventually, his indomitable spirit gained the respect of even the prison guards.

By far the cruelest torment he had to endure was his inability to aid his family or shield them from the incessant persecution of the authorities. The Mandela home was attacked and burned; his wife was repeatedly harassed, arrested and brutally interrogated. Under the apartheid system, the South African government could arbitrarily arrest and detain anyone. This policy claimed countless victims, not least the many black South African children who have grown up missing one or both parents.

Mandela was in prison when he learned that his mother had died of a heart attack. It filled him with immense pain to think that she died still worrying about his safety, as she had throughout the long years of his struggle for freedom and dignity. Shortly thereafter, he was told that his eldest son had been killed in a highly suspect automobile "accident." This was almost too much for even Nelson Mandela to bear. He mourned alone all through the night.

REUNION WITH HOPE

Yet throughout it all, he refused to abandon hope. In 1978, sixteen years into his imprisonment, he was finally able to have a direct meeting with his daughter Zeni. She had married a prince of Swaziland, thus gaining the diplomatic privilege of a face-to-face meeting, without the thick walls and heavy glass that had separated them in the past.

Zeni brought her newborn daughter with her. Embracing his daughter, Mandela felt a charge of emotion: the last time he had hugged his daughter she had been as small as the infant accompanying her that day. Throughout their visit, he held his granddaughter in his arms. As he later wrote: "To hold a newborn baby, so soft and vulnerable, in my rough hands, hands that had for too long only held picks and shovels, was a profound joy. I don't think a man was ever happier to hold a baby than I was that day."

Zeni asked him to name the child. He chose Zaziswe, "Hope." Hope had been his constant companion over the long years, the friend who had remained faithfully by his side in prison. Looking at his granddaughter, he thought of the future and how, when she was grown, apartheid would be a distant memory; of a country not ruled by whites or by blacks, but where all people would live in equality and harmony. He was thinking of her and her generation walking proudly and fearlessly under the sun of freedom. With these thoughts swirling through his mind, he named the tiny baby "Hope."

INVISIBLE HUMANITY

When President Mandela and I first met in 1990, I suggested organizing a series of programs to inform the Japanese public about the realities of apartheid and to promote education in South Africa. President Mandela accepted my proposals with genuine joy. His secretary, Ismail Meer, said that this offer of cultural exchange was a welcome recognition of Africans as human beings. This, he said, is what had been denied them in South Africa, where they were subjected to the indignity of having to register themselves as "blacks." His words brought into new and poignant focus the suffering they had endured.

The tendency to label people is not unique to South Africa. Such prejudiced attitudes are at the root of human rights abuses everywhere. By lumping people into categories, our ability to imagine their thoughts and feelings is stunted. We can no longer put ourselves in their shoes. We stop recognizing them as individuals, as our fellow human beings. They are there in front of us, but we do not see them.

The white minority government was firmly committed to the belief that blacks were an ignorant mass unable to think for themselves. This led to the absurd assumption that any protests must be being instigated and controlled by a small group of leaders. The authorities therefore turned their attack on the leadership of the African National Congress (ANC), which in fact was merely giving voice to the outrage, prayers and hopes of millions of individuals.

DIVIDING THE CONTINENT

An unwillingness to see human realities—to recognize the humanity of the people of Africa—is literally inscribed on the map of modern Africa. Why is it that so many of the national borders of a land of such rich natural, geographic and human diversity should follow straight, geometric lines? Many of these borders have their origin in the 1885 Berlin Conference, also known as the Conference on the Partition of Africa. At this conference, the Great Powers of Europe divided the continent into spheres of influence and colonial holdings—without any consideration for the people actually living there.

Coherent groups of people sharing linguistic and cultural traditions were divided. Societies of cattle herders, for example, who used to travel freely according to grazing conditions, now found themselves on opposite sides of national borders. On the other hand, groups sharing little in common were thrust together in the new political units, a key factor in the subsequent history of civil and international conflict in Africa.

The utterly arbitrary nature of these borders is reflected in the line separating Kenya and Tanzania drawn at the Berlin Conference. The otherwise ruler-straight border jogs slightly to place Mount Kilimanjaro inside Tanzania's territory. There is a long-standing story claiming that this originated when the German Kaiser was asked if he wanted anything for his birthday. He replied that he would like nothing more than several of Africa's snow-capped peaks. Regardless of the historical accuracy of this story, it clearly reflects the attitude of those engaged in the work of dividing up Africa.

Africa is not a "Dark Continent." The darkness was brought from without. Nor is Africa a poor continent. It was made poor by rapacious exploitation. It is not underdeveloped. Its natural development was impeded, like a person whose arms and legs have been severed.

During the Cold War, Africa became a stage for the proxy wars of the Eastern and Western blocs, and the weapons brokers of major powers grew rich as a result. Behind the famines that came to plague the continent were the businesses that monopolized food distribution. This manufactured poverty triggered more internal violence.

And what did the rest of the world have to say to the African people who had endured so much? They called Africa a "failure." What indescribable arrogance!

Knowing this history, the world should by rights unite in an effort to turn Africa, a land of the greatest suffering, into a land of the greatest happiness. For members of our same human family are suffering; they are engaged in a struggle for human dignity.

EQUALITY FOR ALL

"The struggle is my life." True to this conviction, in 1962 Mandela transformed even the courtroom in which he was being tried into a battleground of courageously articulated ideals and eloquent appeals for justice. Standing before the judge, he demanded that the right to vote be extended to all South Africans. He declared, "I consider myself neither legally nor morally bound to obey laws made by a parliament in which I have no representation."

From within his prison cell, Mandela continued to inspire the people of South Africa. Although he was unable to communicate with them, his very existence was a source of hope. The sun continues to shine brightly, no matter how thick the clouds that attempt to obscure it.

The world registered its disgust for apartheid and its support for those resisting it through economic sanctions and cultural and sports boycotts. Feeling this pressure, the South African government on several occasions held out the offer of early release. Mandela consistently refused these offers, which would have compromised the integrity of the movement. He refused to consider his own freedom before that of the whole country had been achieved. In his eyes, all of South Africa was a prison.

"RAINBOW NATION"

At last the day of his release arrived, February 11, 1990. On that day, Mandela addressed a rally in Cape Town. Responding to the rapturous enthusiasm of the crowd, he said:

> I stand here before you not as a prophet but as a humble servant of you, the people. Your tireless and heroic sacrifices have made it possible for me to be here today. I therefore place the remaining years of my life in your hands.

President Mandela dreams of a land ruled neither by blacks nor whites, but of a "rainbow nation" in which all people enjoy equal treatment. He says: "It is an ideal which I hope to live for and to achieve. But if needs be, it is an ideal for which I am prepared to die."

I believe I gained a more intimate sense of what motivates the actions of this great leader during our second meeting. President Mandela told me that he has never forgotten the warm welcome he received from the youthful members of the Soka Gakkai when we met the first time. He made particular mention of their "sparkling eyes." That expression struck me. What was in his heart when he spoke those words?

Could he have been thinking of all those who were deprived of the opportunity to gain an education under apartheid? Students such as Onkgoposte Ramothibi Tiro... Tiro shocked those attending the April 1972 graduation ceremony of the University of the North by openly criticizing the government's racist educational policies, which sought to systematically instill a sense of inferiority in African students. The day would come, he declared, "when all shall be free to breathe the air of freedom which is theirs to breathe and when that day shall come, no man, no matter how many tanks he has, will reverse the course of events."

For speaking out in this way, Tiro was expelled from the university, but he remained active as a leader of the South African Student Movement. On February 4, 1974, while living in exile in neighboring Botswana, he opened a package that had come in the mail. It exploded, killing him. He was 28. His motto had been: "It is better to die for an idea that will live than to live for an idea that will die."

When he became chancellor of the University of the North in 1992, Nelson Mandela praised the courage of the students who had continued to fight apartheid, despite being imprisoned or forced into exile. At the top of this list of such youthful heroes, he named Onkgoposte Ramothibi Tiro.

"THEY ARE WITH ME"

South Africa's first non-racial elections, open to all citizens, were held in April 1994. As Nelson Mandela walked to the voting booth, the faces of all those who had died on the journey to that moment arose in his mind, one after another. Men, women, children, they had given their lives so that he and his fellow South Africans could be where they were that day. "I did not go into that voting station alone on April 27; I was casting my vote with all of them."

The most profound philosophies are born in those who have endured the most severe oppression. In Mandela's own words:

> It was during those long and lonely years that my hunger for the freedom of my own people became a hunger for the freedom of all people, white and black. I knew as well as I knew anything that the oppressor must be liberated just as surely as the oppressed. A man who takes away another man's freedom is a prisoner of hatred, he is locked behind the bars of prejudice and narrow-mindedness... The oppressed and the oppressor alike are robbed of their humanity.

No one can better teach us the deepest meaning of freedom than this man who spent half his adult life imprisoned. The essence of freedom is found in immovable conviction. Only those who live true to their convictions, whose inner faith enables them to rise above the fetters of any situation, are truly free. As President Mandela says: "To be free is not merely to cast off one's chains, but to live in a way that respects and enhances the freedom of others."

The struggle President Mandela has waged to bring apartheid to an end—his struggle for human rights for all—is really the struggle of all humanity. It is a struggle for the very soul of human dignity. I feel that he and his fellow champions of freedom in South Africa took up this struggle as the representatives of, and on behalf of, the entire human race.

VALENTINA TERESHKOVA

First Woman in Space

Valentina Tereshkova (1937–), Russia

The first woman to orbit the Earth, in the Soviet spaceship Vostok VI in June 1963, Valentina Tereshkova was born near Yaroslavl in Central Russia where she worked in a textile mill and was active in the local Air Sports Club. In 1962 she was selected to begin cosmonaut training. After her experience in space, Tereshkova's political career spanned periods as chair of the Soviet Women's Committee and as head of the Union of Soviet Societies for Friendship and Cultural Relations with Foreign Countries.

Valentina Tereshkova

First Woman in Space

"You cannot possibly imagine how beautiful it is. Anyone who sees Earth from outer space, even once, cannot fail to be overwhelmed by a sense of reverence and love for this planet that is our home." Valentina Tereshkova was the first woman in space, orbiting Earth in Vostok 6 in June 1963 at the age of only 26. Her lively voice was broadcast to people all around the world: "It is I, Seagull!" Using her call sign Chaika (Seagull), she reported: "I see the horizon—a light blue, a beautiful band. The Earth—it is so beautiful!" The image of a seagull soaring on high seemed to fit the young cosmonaut perfectly, and she came to be known affectionately as "Seagull" by people everywhere.

I first met Ms. Tereshkova in Moscow in May 1975, during my second visit to the Soviet Union. Seated facing me with a warm smile of welcome, in her green sweater and brown cardigan, she seemed modest and unassuming. I asked her why she had become a cosmonaut, curious to know what had caused her to embark on such an exciting adventure. "Let me see…," she began in a quiet voice, hands folded on the table. Her eyes, which had gazed down on Earth from space, were blue like the Earth, shining with earnest sincerity.

Ms. Tereshkova told me that her desire to voyage into space was sparked by the example of Soviet cosmonaut Yuri Gagarin, who succeed-

ed in making the first manned space flight on April 12, 1961. The whole
world was talking about his epoch-making achievement, nowhere more so
than the Soviet Union: "The first man in space! A Soviet youth! One of
ours!" The factory where she worked was filled with an air of excitement and
jubilation; it was a day of festive celebration. Returning home that evening,
young Valentina's life was changed forever by her mother's seemingly casual
remark: "Now that a man has gone into space, it's a woman's turn."

THE SCARS OF WAR

Ms. Tereshkova was raised by her mother. When she was two, her
father went off to fight in World War II and was killed in action soon after.
He had been a tractor driver, and she has only faint memories of him giving her a ride on his tractor.

The news of his death arrived on a blizzard-tossed night. The sight of
her mother quietly sobbing stays with her, like a bad dream, to this day. She
was only three. She had one older sister and her mother was pregnant with
her brother. Her grandmother, unable to accept the fact that her son had
died, never stopped waiting for his return. What untold pain and suffering
has been inflicted on women and children by war! I, and those of my generation, have witnessed this reality to a truly unbearable extent.

A widow at 27, Ms. Tereshkova's mother did her best to support and
raise her three children on her own, leaving for work each day before
dawn. At times she would say that their entire family must have been abandoned by fortune: of her own seven siblings, three had died of starvation
and two had been killed in internal conflict within the Soviet Union.

Eventually the family moved to the city. Her mother and sister
worked at a textile mill in Yaroslavl, on the banks of the Volga. Her
mother was so busy that none of the children remember ever seeing her
take a moment to rest or relax. At 17, Ms. Tereshkova herself went to
work in a tire factory. On her first payday, she bought a flower-print head
scarf and some sweets for her mother. When her mother saw the gifts,
she burst into tears.

Following Gagarin's historic space flight, the space program was opened to all Soviet citizens. "I volunteered, of course," Ms. Tereshkova told me. "I'm sure there wasn't a single young person in all of the Soviet Union who wouldn't have given anything to be able to do what Lieutenant Gagarin had done," she says of that time.

She had the good fortune to be chosen as a candidate, but the training was much more strenuous than she had anticipated. She didn't go into detail, saying only: "The training was very tough, in both kind and quantity. It progressed stage by stage, each one a real challenge to my physical strength." One can easily imagine how demanding the training really must have been; she once wrote that when she was being spun in the centrifuge, which simulates the stresses of extreme acceleration and deceleration, she felt as if her blood had turned to mercury.

In addition to physical training, she engaged in intensive study of a range of specialized subjects including, of course, rocket science. Each day was a battle, but she was not deterred: "I believe that when you have a dream and commit yourself body and soul to realizing it, you can achieve it without fail." She kept a picture of her mother in her room and her mother's gaze seemed to encourage her: "I know you can do it!" Whenever she received her salary, she would hurry to the post office to send money home.

MOTHERS' PRAYERS

The day finally arrived when she would actually go into space. Over the course of three days, she orbited the Earth forty-eight times—meaning that she saw a new dawn every one and a half hours. "It was breathtakingly beautiful," she said, "like something out of a fairy tale." Earth is surrounded by a layer of soft, constantly shifting light that displays all the colors of the rainbow. "There is no way I can describe the joy of seeing the Earth," she remarked. "It was blue, and far more beautiful than any of the other stars or planets. Each continent, every ocean, had its own distinct beauty."

As she circled the Earth, she thought of her mother back home. She thought of all the mothers on Earth. The planet was teeming with life. She saw mountains and thought of the birds living there. Forests came into view and she thought of all the animals and insects to whom these are home. Rivers and oceans filled with fish… And they all had mothers, as do all the people on Earth.

She realized that every single person on Earth has a mother who has gone through the pain of childbirth to bring them into the world. She thought of each child as a prince or princess of Earth, whose birth had been blessed and celebrated. If the Earth's mothers had even once stopped nurturing their children, none of us would be here. From mother to child, mother to child—if even once this millennial chain of life had been completely severed, we would not be here today. She reflected on the infinite number of mothers—mothers who wish only that we, their children, will enjoy healthy, happy lives.

She couldn't help feeling that Earth is filled with the sound of these mothers' prayers. Gazing down from space, Ms. Tereshkova thought: "There are all sorts of mothers on our planet, but to me, mine is the best. I want to make sure that there are no more war widows like my mother, and no more children like me, who never knew their own fathers."

The Earth gives birth to life. States kill. The Earth nurtures life. Governments command people to discard their lives. If states and nations are the territory of men, then Earth itself, far larger than any single country, belongs to mothers. It is the stage where their nurturing love for life itself is enacted. We must make the 21st century a century of life, a century of women. We must make it an age when the prayers for peace of all mothers, prayers as old as human history, are finally answered.

My friendship with Ms. Tereshkova continues to this day. In May 1987, I was invited to the Soviet Union by the Presidium of the Union of Soviet Societies for Friendship and Cultural Relations with Foreign Countries, which she chaired. On that occasion, she was not only kind enough to greet me at the airport but also accompanied me to various functions over a four-day period. The SGI had brought its "Nuclear Weapons: Threat to

Our World" exhibition to Moscow and Ms. Tereshkova was there very early on the opening day, busily helping with preparations.

"Once you've been in space, you appreciate how small and fragile Earth is. This small, blue, shining planet. We must not allow it to be covered by the black ash of a nuclear war. All the women of the world must join hands and make peace happen. We are all riding on 'Spaceship Earth' together."

Seagull continues her flight, pursuing the dream of peace.

Mahatma Gandhi

The Courage of Nonviolence

MOHANDAS KARAMCHAND GANDHI (1869–1948), INDIA
KNOWN POPULARLY AS THE MAHATMA (GREAT SOUL)

After qualifying as a lawyer in London in 1891, Gandhi moved to South Africa where he began his political career lobbying against racially discriminatory laws. Returning to India during World War I, he played a key role in winning India's independence from Britain through his advocacy and practice of satyagraha *(nonviolent protest) as a means of revolution. Gandhi's principles and example have inspired countless activists including Martin Luther King, Jr. and Nelson Mandela. He was assassinated during the political turmoil following the post-independence partitioning of India.*

MAHATMA GANDHI

The Courage of Nonviolence

―✦―

I don't want toys or chocolate. All I want is peace and freedom. People of Europe, people of the world, please find the humanity in your hearts to put an end to this war! —A young girl from the former Yugoslavia

I was visiting Raj Ghat, where Mahatma Gandhi, the father of Indian independence, had been cremated. Somewhere a bird sang. A forest was nearby, and squirrels ran through its lush green thickets.

The area was a spacious, well-tended shrine to nonviolence. As I offered flowers before the black stone platform that constitutes Gandhi's memorial, I bowed my head.

I pondered Gandhi's brilliant spirit. I thought of his ceaseless struggles to douse the fires of hatred with water drawn from the pure springs of love for humanity.

And I thought of how alone he was in his quest.

"WHOSE SIDE ARE YOU ON?"

"Gandhi tells us not to retaliate against the Muslims! How can he take their side? There's no way! They killed my family, including my five-year-old son!"

"Is he telling us just to endure the attacks of the Hindus? Ridiculous! Doesn't he know what we Muslims have been through all these years? After all, Gandhi's a Hindu himself, isn't he?"

The year was 1947. The partition of the newly-independent India along religious lines was accompanied by enormous disruption and violence. The elderly sage went everywhere, wherever Hindus and Muslims were mired in blood-stained cycles of conflict and reprisal. He called for the killing to end. But people, crazed by hate, did not listen. They told him to leave, calling his attempts at reconciliation hypocritical or worse. They demanded to know whose side he was on.

But he wasn't on either side. And at the same time, he was on both sides. To him, people are brothers and sisters. How could he stand by, a silent witness to mutual slaughter?

Gandhi declared that he was willing to be cut in two if that was what people wanted, but not for India to be cut in two. What good, he demanded to know, could ever come of hatred? If hate was returned with hate, it would only become more deeply rooted and widespread.

Suppose someone sets fire to your home and you retaliate by setting fire to theirs, soon the whole town will be in flames! Burning down the attacker's house won't bring yours back. Violence solves nothing. By engaging in reprisals, you only hurt yourself.

But no matter how urgently Gandhi called on people to listen to reason, the fires of hatred raged on. Against the lone Gandhi there were far too many people fanning the flames.

FIRE CANNOT EXTINGUISH FIRE

On January 20, 1948—ten days, in fact, before he was assassinated— a handmade bomb was hurled at Gandhi as he attended a gathering. This act of terrorism was carried out by a Hindu youth. Fortunately, the bomb missed the mark and Gandhi survived. The youth was arrested.

The next day, several adherents of the Sikh faith called on Gandhi and assured him that the culprit was not a Sikh.

Gandhi rebuked them, saying that it mattered nothing at all to him whether the assailant was a Sikh, a Hindu or a Muslim.

Whoever the perpetrator might be, he said, he wished him well.

Gandhi explained that the youth had been taught to think of him as an enemy of the Hindu cause, that hatred had been implanted in his heart. The youth believed what he was taught and was so desperate, so devoid of all hope, that violence seemed the only alternative.

Gandhi felt only pity for the young man. He even told the outraged chief of police to not harass his assailant but make an effort to convert him to right thoughts and actions. This was always his approach. No one abhorred violence more than Gandhi. At the same time no one knew more deeply that violence can only be countered by nonviolence.

Just as fire is extinguished by water, hatred can only be defeated by love and compassion. Some criticized Gandhi for coddling the terrorist. Others scorned his conviction, calling it sentimental and unrealistic, an empty vision.

Gandhi was alone.

Many revered his name, but few truly shared his beliefs. For Gandhi, nonviolence meant an overflowing love for all humanity, a way of life that emanated from the very marrow of his being. It made life possible; without it, he could not have lived even a moment. But for many of his followers, nonviolence was simply a political strategy, a tactic for winning India's independence from Britain.

Gandhi was alone.

The more earnestly he pursued his religious beliefs, the deeper his love for humanity grew. This love made it all the more impossible for him to ignore the political realities that shaped people's lives. At the same time, contact with these political realities strengthened his conviction that nothing is more essential than the love for all humanity that religious faith can inspire.

This placed him, however, in the position of being denounced by both religious figures, who saw his involvement in the sullied realm of politics as driven by personal ambition, and political leaders, who called him ignorant and naïve.

Because he walked the middle way, the true path of humanity that seeks to reconcile apparent contradictions, his beliefs and actions appeared biased to those at the extremes.

ENDING TERROR

The September 11, 2001, attacks against the United States were savage beyond words. Members of the Soka Gakkai International were among the victims. The attacks provoked universal revulsion and the heartfelt desire that such slaughter never be repeated.

For what crime were these innocent people killed? There is no reason, nothing that could possibly justify such an act. Even if the perpetrators believed they were acting based on their religious faith, their acts in no way merit the name of martyrdom. Martyrdom means offering up one's own life, not taking the lives of others. True self-sacrifice is made to save others from suffering, to offer them happiness. Any act that involves killing others is reprehensible and purely destructive.

The time has come for humankind to join together to put an end to terrorism. The question is, how can this be achieved? Can military retaliation serve that end? Isn't it likely only to incite more hatred?

Even if, for argument's sake, the immediate "enemy" could be subdued, would that bring true peace? Long-simmering hatreds would only be driven further underground, making it impossible to predict where next in the world they might burst forth. We risk creating a world tormented with ever-greater fear and unease.

Here I am reminded of the simple wisdom of the Aesop fable "The North Wind and the Sun." The North Wind tried to make a traveler remove his coat by assailing him with icy gusts, but the harder the North Wind blew, the tighter the traveler pulled his coat around him.

Peace that is based on the forceful suppression of people's voices and concerns, whether it be in our own or other countries, is a dead peace—the peace of the grave. Surely that is not the peace for which humanity yearns.

VIOLENCE VS. NONVIOLENCE

I am also reminded of a moving episode that Leo Tolstoy related in a letter written two months before his death. The letter, dated September 7, 1910, was addressed to Mahatma Gandhi.

The episode went something like this. There was a test on the subject of religion in a certain girls' school in Moscow. A bishop had come to the school and was quizzing the girls one by one about the Ten Commandments. When he came to the commandment "Thou shalt not kill," the bishop asked: "Does God forbid us to kill under all circumstances?"

The girls each answered as they had been taught. "No," they said, "not under all circumstances. We may kill in war or as legal punishment."

"Yes, that's right! You've answered correctly!" said the bishop. Then one of the girls, her face flushed with indignation, spoke up: "Killing is wrong under all circumstances!"

The bishop was flustered and marshaled all his rhetorical skills to convince the girl that there were exceptions to the commandment against killing, but to no avail.

"No," she declared. "Killing is a sin under all circumstances. It says so in the Old Testament. Moreover, Jesus not only forbade killing but taught that we must do no harm to our neighbors."

In the face of truth in the girl's assertion, the bishop's authority and verbal skills were of no use whatsoever. In the end, he could only fall silent. The young girl, Tolstoy wrote with evident satisfaction, had proven victorious.

Let us amplify the words of that young girl "It is wrong to kill, even in war!" And let us broadcast them to the world!

The 20th century was a century of war, a century in which hundreds of millions of people died violent deaths. Have we learned anything from those horrific tragedies? In the new era of the 21st century, humanity must be guided by the overriding principle that killing is never acceptable or justified—under any circumstance. Unless we realize this, unless we widely promote and deeply implant the understanding that violence can never be used to advocate one's beliefs, we will have learned nothing from the bitter lessons of the 20th century.

The real struggle of the 21st century will not be between civilizations, nor between religions. It will be between violence and nonviolence. It will be between barbarity and civilization in the truest sense of the word.

A FLOOD OF DIALOGUE

More than half a century ago, Gandhi sought to break the cycles of violence and reprisal. What distinguishes us from brute beasts, he said, is our continuous striving for moral self-improvement. Humanity is at a crossroads and must choose, he asserted, violence (the law of the jungle) or nonviolence (the law of humanity).

The world today, in fact, has an extraordinary and unprecedented opportunity. We have the chance to open a new page in human history. Now is the time to make the following declaration:

We regard terrorist attacks to be a challenge to the law of humanity. It is for just this reason that we refuse to follow the law of the jungle upon which the attacks were based. We declare our determination to find a solution not by military means but through extensive dialogue. Rather than further fuel the flames of hatred, we choose to douse them with a great "flood of dialogue" that will enrich and benefit all humanity.

This is the best, the only means to assure that such horrors are never repeated, and we believe it is the most fitting way to honor the memory of those who lost their lives in the attacks.

Such a declaration, put into action, would certainly be met with the unstinting praise of future historians.

Great good can come of great evil. But this will not happen on its own. Courage is always required to transform evil into good. Now is the time for each of us to bring forth such courage: the courage of nonviolence, the courage of dialogue, the courage to listen to what we would rather not hear, the courage to restrain the desire for vengeance and be guided by reason.

A WILLINGNESS TO LISTEN

In conversations with Mrs. Veena Sikri, director general of the Indian Council for Cultural Relations, we discussed Indian philosophy and the tradition of nonviolence. And I spoke of my desire to bring the light of India, with its immense spiritual heritage, to the people of Japan. This wish was eventually realized in the form of an exhibition entitled "King Ashoka, Mahatma Gandhi, and Nehru—Healing Touch" that was held in Japan in 1994.

King Ashoka was a wise and virtuous monarch of ancient India (around the third century B.C.E.). After witnessing firsthand the cruel realities of war, he converted to Buddhism, deciding that he would base his rule not on military force but on the Dharma, the principles of Buddhism. When Gandhi was asked whether a nonviolent state was possible, he replied that indeed it was. He pointed to Ashoka's reign as an example, and asserted that it must be possible to reproduce the ancient king's achievement.

Jawaharlal Nehru, the first prime minister of independent India, was Gandhi's direct disciple. When he visited Japan in 1957, he voiced his profound concern over the escalating violence in the world. In one of his addresses he stated that the only truly effective response to the hydrogen bomb was not a bomb of even bigger destructive capacity but a spiritual "bomb" of compassion. This was just one month after Josei Toda, the second president of the Soka Gakkai, made his own declaration calling for the abolition of nuclear weapons.

Some of the Japanese involved in preparing for the "King Ashoka, Mahatma Gandhi, and Nehru" exhibition at first had difficulty appreciating the "healing touch" theme proposed by our Indian partners. This may have been partly because "healing" in the broader sense was not as familiar a term in Japan as it has since become. But no theme goes more to the very heart of nonviolence. For violence is born from a wounded spirit: a spirit burned and blistered by the fire of arrogance; a spirit splintered and frayed by the frustration of powerlessness; a spirit parched with an unquenched thirst for meaning in life; a spirit shriveled and shrunk by feelings of inferiority. The rage that results from injured self-respect, from humiliation, erupts as violence. A culture of violence, which delights in crushing and beating others into submission, spreads throughout society, often amplified by the media.

The American civil rights leader Dr. Martin Luther King, Jr., was a student of Gandhi's philosophy. He declared that a person whose spirit is in turmoil cannot truly practice nonviolence. It was my hope that the light of India—a country known in the East since ancient times as "the land of moonlight"—would help spread the spirit of peace, much as the cool beams of the moon bring soothing relief from the maddening heat of the day. From a healed, peaceful heart, humility is born; from humility, a willingness to listen to others is born; from a willingness to listen to others, mutual understanding is born; and from mutual understanding, a peaceful society will be born.

Nonviolence is the highest form of humility; it is supreme courage. Prime Minister Nehru said that the essence of Gandhi's teachings was fearlessness. The Mahatma taught that "the strong are never vindictive" and that dialogue can only be engaged in by the brave.

My Reminiscences

A Piece of Mirror

A Piece of Mirror

Reminiscences of the author's childhood in wartime Japan and the key influence of his elder brother Kiichi.

My Reminiscences

A Piece of Mirror

⸺⸹⸺

My mother was an ordinary Japanese woman like many other women born in the late 19th century. She devoted herself to her rather difficult husband, and raised eight children—seven boys and a girl. I was the fifth son. There were also two foster children, making a total of ten. Her life was by no means an easy one. My father, who died in 1956, was so hardheaded and obstinate that he was known among his relatives and neighbors as "Old Dichard." I know my mother must have had enormous patience to stick with him until the end of his life.

When she married, my mother brought a mirror stand fitted with a beautiful, decorative mirror as part of her trousseau. Twenty years later, however, the mirror somehow broke. My eldest brother Kiichi and I sorted over the thick fragments and carefully picked out two of the larger ones to keep.

Not long after that war erupted. My four elder brothers one by one went off to the front, some to fight in China, others in Southeast Asia. My brothers, who were in the prime of life, ready to work and contribute to our family, were taken from us, each by a single piece of paper—the conscription notice. My mother tried not to show her grief, but she seemed to age suddenly.

HATRED OF WAR

I will never forget the disgust and anger with which Kiichi, on leave from China, described the inhuman atrocities he had seen committed there by the Japanese Imperial Army. Japan was wrong, he said, and he felt deeply for Chinese people. Listening to his words, I developed a profound hatred for war, its cruelty, stupidity and waste. And although I was only in grade school, I remember determining that in the future I would somehow work to bring about reconciliation between the people of China and Japan.

Later the air raids in Tokyo began, and soon they were a daily occurrence. I kept my piece of mirror with me always. I dodged my way through the fire-bombs that fell all around us with it safely tucked in a breast pocket. Kiichi had set off to the front once more, and we all missed his cheerful presence.

In March 1944, as the bombing of Tokyo intensified, my family was ordered to evacuate the house in which I had grown up, as it had to be torn down to make a fire break. Just as we had managed to move all the family belongings into my aunt's house and were ready to move ourselves, an air raid targeted my aunt's neighborhood. Her home took a direct hit and burned to the ground. The only thing my younger brother and I managed to pull from the flames was an old trunk. In the hazy light of the next morning, we opened this trunk, our sole remaining possession.

Inside was a single umbrella and a collection of large decorative dolls usually displayed in Japan on the day of the Girls Festival, March 3. Of all the useless things to survive the flames! We moaned in disappointment. Even though she must have shared our deep frustration, my mother refused to give in to it. "I'm sure that we'll come to live in the kind of home where we can display these dolls properly," she had said. "I'm certain of it." Her words provoked a smile, then laughter and hope.

The war had cast its shadow into every corner of our lives. Finally, the end that we all knew was coming had arrived: Defeat. On August 15, 1945, the war, which had been started and fought in the Emperor's name, now ended with the Emperor's voice on the radio—a "sacred" voice we had never before heard—urging the Japanese people to "bear the unbearable." At 17, my heart was torn between hope and anxiety.

People just sat around in a daze. But then we realized that the skies were quiet for the first time in months. A sense of relief seemed to spread. That night we were allowed to turn the lights on at last. How bright! I thought—what a good thing peace is. We were all relieved, but no one dared come right out and say, "I'm glad we lost."

My mother's only wish, her only hope, was for the safe return of her sons. She was particularly worried about Kiichi. We hadn't heard a word from him since he reported having left China for Southeast Asia. From time to time, my mother would tell us that she'd seen Kiichi in a dream, and that he'd told her that he would soon return.

Eventually, nearly two years after the war ended and my other brothers had returned, one by one, we received notification that Kiichi had been killed in Burma. I thought at once of the piece of mirror I knew he carried in the breast pocket of his uniform. I could imagine him, during a lull in the fighting, taking it out and looking at his unshaven face in it, thinking longingly of mother at home.

THE GREATEST LOSS

It was on May 30, 1947, that we received the news of Kiichi's death in the form of a letter brought by an elderly local official. We had moved after having been burned out of our home, and apparently it had been no easy matter to track us down. My mother bowed politely and accepted the letter. She turned her back to us, shuddering with grief. One of my older brothers went to pick up Kiichi's cremated remains. I couldn't bear to look at my mother as she stood clasping the small white box that held all that was left of her eldest child. This was the greatest loss, the deepest sadness she experienced in her life. I felt, in the depths of my being, the tragedy and cruel waste of war.

In the dark and troubled times after Japan's defeat, I left home and moved into my own lodgings. The room I rented was small, bare and ugly, but fortunately I had my piece of broken mirror with me. Every morning before I went to work I would take it out and use it while I shaved and combed my hair.

In 1952, when I married, my wife Kaneko brought along with her a brand-new mirror stand, and from then on I looked at my face in the new mirror. One day I found Kaneko with the piece of old mirror in her hand and a look of puzzlement on her face. When I saw that the mirror was likely to end up in the trash basket if I didn't speak up, I told her about the history attached to it. Somewhere she managed to find a small box of fine paulownia wood, and she stored the piece of mirror away in it. It's still safe in its box today.

The piece of broken mirror, whenever I look at it, speaks to me about those far-off days of my youth, my mother's prayers, and the sad fate of my eldest brother. It will continue to do so as long as I live.

CHINGIZ AITMATOV

The Writer's Path

CHINGIZ AITMATOV (1928–), KYRGYZSTAN

Renowned writer and politician Chingiz Aitmatov was adviser to then Soviet president Mikhail Gorbachev from 1990 to 1991. Growing up in rural Kyrgyzstan, he first trained as a livestock specialist, then studied literature and became a correspondent for Pravda. *Themes in his writing include the tensions between the cultural heritage of the peoples of Central Asia and the Soviet ways, particularly as they affected women. He is currently ambassador of the Kyrgyz Republic based in Belgium.*

CHINGIZ AITMATOV

The Writer's Path

⟶⟵

In the autumn of 1937, when he was eight years old, Chingiz Aitmatov boarded a train at Moscow's Kazan Station with his mother, younger brother and two younger sisters. His father came to see them off.

"Why are we leaving?" Chingiz wondered. He couldn't figure out why his father was suddenly sending them all back home to Kyrgyzstan. His father, a respected figure in his community, was a leader in the newly formed Kyrgyz Communist Party. He had come to Moscow with his family to study.

But the Stalinist purges, which are said to have claimed the lives of tens of millions, had begun. Sensing danger, his father was determined to ensure the family's safety.

Young Aitmatov's father walked alongside the train with his palm pressed against the window as it began to pull out. As it gathered speed, he started running and continued in stride with the train, right to the end of the platform, as if to prolong his farewell to the last possible moment. His children innocently waved good-bye to him, unaware of the significance of the moment. Mr. Aitmatov remembers that the day was September 1. He recalls it every time he passes Kazan Station. "Father, you knew that was our final farewell…"

Kyrgyzstan is a beautiful land, with vast grasslands and the Tien Shan Mountains ranging high into the clear blue skies. It is blessed with crystal streams, azure lakes shimmering with silver waves; its green hills are blanketed with poplars, and the night skies glow with countless stars.

In the midst of all this natural beauty, in the remote village that was their home, the Aitmatov family had to live as virtual outcasts.

When Chingiz's mother asked the Party what had become of her husband, she was told he was sentenced to 10 years in prison without permission to write or receive letters. That, of course, was a lie. He had already been executed, just two months after their farewell at the station. He was only 35.

LEARNING PRIDE

When the family returned to Kyrgyzstan, the youngest child was only six months old. Though their mother was in poor health, she had to shoulder the full weight of caring for her family. She raised her children while working as an accountant for one of the local collective farms. Chingiz Aitmatov worked in the fields from the time he was a child.

The neighbors cast a cold eye on the family, who didn't even dare speak their father's name out loud. Many villagers assumed that since their father was being punished he must have done something bad. There were times when the young Aitmatov didn't even want to tell people his last name.

But there were some in the village who did not allow their vision to be clouded by the swirl of events. One was an elementary school teacher who said to Chingiz: "Never look down when you say your father's name. Do you understand?" These words became a lifelong treasure to him.

"That teacher gave me courage," Mr. Aitmatov says. "It was impossible to imagine in those days someone telling me to be proud of my disgraced father. My teacher taught me to hold fast to my humanity and to place utmost importance on the value of human dignity. Even now, my blood boils whenever I see someone being demeaned or insulted."

A DAUNTLESS SPIRIT

I first met Mr. Aitmatov in Tokyo in 1988, when he was traveling the world as a spokesperson for the *perestroika* reforms of President Mikhail Gorbachev. Later he became a member of the Soviet Presidential Council, where he was a supporter of the humanistic political philosophy known as "new thinking." The moment I shook hands with him, I intuitively felt that he was a man of lion-like courage. His countenance revealed a dauntless spirit. He exuded an air of great strength, passion and sensitivity.

Chingiz Aitmatov was born in December 1928, the same year as myself. "Our generation," he says, "experienced war when we were young. We have seen what terrible suffering war causes and the starvation and grief war brings. We have also seen how people rise from the ashes of destruction in search of the light of a new age."

When World War II began, all the able-bodied men in Mr. Aitmatov's village went off to fight. Only the elderly, women and children remained. The Aitmatovs' life grew even more difficult. They lived in a dilapidated mud-brick shack that had been abandoned.

Struggling against poor health, Mrs. Aitmatov was unable to send all four children to school, so Chingiz had to quit school at 14. But because he excelled in reading and writing, he was chosen to be secretary of the village council. In this capacity, he had to collect taxes from the villagers. This was a truly onerous task for a 14-year-old, as many of the families had lost their main breadwinners and didn't have enough to eat.

But the job he hated most was delivering the official death notices to the families of soldiers killed in action. When he appeared at the homes of those who had loved ones at the front, they would peer at him with frightened, anxious faces. He would take out of his bag a small piece of paper roughly the size of the palm of his hand bearing the seal of the Soviet army. He had to read out the brief message and then translate it into Kyrgyz.

The mothers would give a heavy sigh that he said sounded like "a mountain of stone collapsing." A sigh that was filled with a rush of unbearable sorrow as if to say: "Ah, my son will never return! I will never embrace him again… That my son should be reduced to this piece of paper!" The young Aitmatov dared not look up but he could not leave. He had no words of comfort to offer them. All he could do was stand there in front of the grieving mother, while an unquenchable anger rose in his heart. Why, he needed to know, were people killing each other? For whom? Are nations nothing more than furnaces that consume people as fuel? And what force had consumed and robbed him of his father?

Since that first encounter, we have met many times. Moscow in the early summer. Tokyo in the autumn. In the mountains north of Tokyo in the summer. Luxembourg in the spring. We have also met in France, as well as in Kyoto. Over the course of wide-ranging discussions, we have found we agree on many issues: The enemy of the people is totalitarianism, whether of the left or right. It is blind and narrow-minded nationalism. It is bureaucracy and authoritarianism. It is the unscrupulous commercialism that will do anything to turn a profit. It is every variety of fanaticism.

MURDEROUS RAGE

Chingiz Aitmatov has come to these views through difficult, often bitter experiences. When he was a boy, there was one incident that angered him to the core and put murder in his heart.

During their years in Kyrgyzstan the Aitmatov family had a cow that they depended upon for milk. It was practically the family's only possession. A relative had given it to them to ease their hunger and poverty. The four children lovingly tended the cow whom they named Zukhra. They looked forward to spring, for in spring they would be able to drink Zukhra's delicious fresh milk. They would even be able to make sour cream.

But one morning when he made his way to the cowshed in the cold wind, Chingiz was startled to find that Zukhra was missing. She had been stolen! It was a tremendous shock for the entire family, as if the earth had given way beneath them. They were too stunned to do anything but weep.

Their mother was suffering from severe asthma and rheumatism.

"How could someone steal the cow that was our only hope! What more suffering must my mother endure? How are we to live…?"

The boy's heart was filled with rage at the thief. "No! I won't let this happen! I will find the thief and kill him!" He borrowed a rifle from a neighbor and set out in the snow and wind to find the thief, trekking across fields and valleys. But the culprit was nowhere to be found. This only made the boy more furious.

As he tramped through the snow, wild-eyed with anger, he came upon an old man on a donkey. The old man was wearing ragged clothes and clearly very poor. He had a long white beard. It was the custom in Kyrgyzstan for young people to greet their elders with respect when they encountered them on the road, but Chingiz was beyond civilities. The old man addressed him instead.

"Hold on, young man! You're not going off to kill someone, are you?"

"Yes, I am."

Their eyes met. The old man looked at him with a warm and gentle gaze. The boy told him the whole sorry tale. After hearing him out, the old man said: "I understand how you feel. My heart, my very bones, ache to see you in this state. But young man, you must not kill, not even in your mind. No matter who it is, not even a vile thief. Their likes will be punished in the course of life.

"If you return home and forget about killing, you will be blessed with happiness. You may not notice it at first, but happiness will come to dwell in your heart. You may think what I'm telling you is just a lot of foolishness right now, but trust me and go home. All right? You must never kill people! You must never even think about killing. Someday you will understand what I'm telling you. Now, young man, go home!"

And with that the old man went on his way.

For some reason, Chingiz did as he was told. After going a short way, he turned around to look back, but the old man was already a small figure in the distance.

Chingiz Aitmatov set off for home, the now-useless rifle weighing heavily on his shoulder. The empty, snow-covered fields sparkled in the sunlight. Tears ran down his cheeks unchecked and loud, shuddering sobs wracked his body as he made his way home.

Writing Rooted in People's Lives

Suffering gave strength, depth and breadth to the boy's spirit. "When I was very young, I saw life from a bright, poetic perspective," says Mr. Aitmatov. "But then it revealed its harsh, raw, painful and heroic aspects to me."

As the secretary of the local council, the young Aitmatov knew every house and family in the village in the most intimate detail. Through his encounters with many people, he acquired practical wisdom that would be useful to him throughout his life. He learned not so much from words as from the lives and example of ordinary people who lived by the sweat of their brows. Gradually and unconsciously, the life and spirit of the people took root in his heart, later finding expression in his writing.

Now, no matter what grand surroundings he finds himself in, Mr. Aitmatov never forgets where he came from. He never forgets the profound debt he owes to the working people who made him who he is.

He believes that in some respects we should all remain "country folk" at heart. We should never lose the smell of the earth, he says, for it is in that very earth that the delicate blossoms of the spirit bloom.

From childhood, his paternal grandmother told him the ancient tales and legends of the people of the steppes and sang to him the old folk songs. When he grew older, he looked for answers to his questions about life in the works of great writers. After World War II, he graduated from the Kyrgyz Agricultural Institute and worked as a livestock specialist. Still, he found himself increasingly drawn to literature; at the age of 27, he entered the Institute of Literature, attached to the Soviet Writers Federation in Moscow.

Published when he was 29, his novella *Jamilya* came to the attention of the French author Louis Aragon, who praised it as "the most beautiful love story in the world." At 34, he was awarded the prestigious Lenin Prize for literature. His works have been translated into many languages and are admired and enjoyed by readers around the world.

Writing has always been a struggle for Mr. Aitmatov. Each word is like a drop of blood. But the authorities played havoc with the words that were the very essence of his being. His wife, Maria, told me about these trials. "During the Soviet era," she said, "everything published had to be approved by the KGB. I often went with my husband to see the censors. They would say, 'You have to cut here and here' or 'Take out this line.' He had to agree to their demands or the entire book would be rejected."

"The responsibility of a writer," Chingiz Aitmatov states, "is to bring forth words that capture, through painful personal experience, people's suffering, pain, faith and hope. This is because a writer is charged with the mission of speaking on behalf of his fellow human beings. Everything that happens in the world happens to me personally."

THE SUMMER OF '91

Mr. Aitmatov knew nothing of his father's fate for decades. When his mother died, some 30 years after they had said farewell to his father at the station, Mr. Aitmatov had her tombstone engraved to say that they both rested there.

Then, twenty years later, his father's remains were discovered.

In August 1991, Soviet President Mikhail Gorbachev and his family were placed under house arrest during an attempted coup d'état. These were the "three days that shook the world" that ultimately led to the collapse of the Soviet Union. It was just before this incident that the remains of Mr. Aitmatov's father were found.

A mass grave containing 138 bodies, identified as victims executed by Stalin in 1937, was uncovered on the site of a former brick factory in

Kyrgyzstan. Because of the passage of time, the victim's clothes and shoes had completely disintegrated. But among the remains a piece of paper pierced with a bullet hole was found. It was a written indictment on which the name Trekul Aitmatov was clearly legible. After 54 years, Aitmatov was finally reunited with his father.

His heart cried out in anguish for his father who had been arrested on false charges and murdered by lies, and for his mother who had endured all, dying without knowing what had become of her husband. His heart surged with anger toward craven liars, toward the lust for power and domination that drives men to madness, toward all those who would inflict such pain and misery on mothers and children.

"In the end, what is right? What should be the standard for distinguishing between right and wrong? I have to believe that it is love for our fellow human beings, for all who have been born on this planet, a love that wishes each person happiness and freedom. No ideology or national framework is more important than this. It is when people love that they become true heroes."

Rabbi Marvin Hier

The Courage to Remember

RABBI MARVIN HIER (1939–), UNITED STATES

Rabbi Marvin Hier is the dean and founder of the Simon Wiesenthal Center (and its acclaimed Museum of Tolerance), an international Jewish human rights organization dedicated to fostering tolerance and understanding. In pursuing the agenda of the Center, he regularly engages in dialogue with world leaders. Rabbi Hier is also the recipient of two Academy Awards as co-producer of the films Genocide *and* Echoes That Remain, *which document the Holocaust and the plight of its survivors.*

Rabbi Marvin Hier

The Courage to Remember

—❧—

R abbi Marvin Hier founded the Simon Wiesenthal Center vowing that those who died in the Holocaust would never be forgotten. He would not allow them to be forgotten.

It has not been an easy task. People want to forget—not only those who perpetrated evil but even, at times, the victims. As Rabbi Hier points out: "Memory is fragile and pliable. And that is why if we do not persist on our course, if we are not faithful to memory, then one day no one will believe that the eerie sounds of those trains once delivered millions of unsuspecting men, women and children to the death camps."

Forget Me Not

Passing through the rotunda of the Simon Wiesenthal Center's new Museum of Tolerance, Rabbi Hier pointed to a small notebook in a glass case. "This poem is in Anne Frank's own handwriting," he said. She wrote it for a friend when she was only ten years old:

> *Dearest Henny,*
> *It is only a small thing*
> *But I give it to you*
> *The roses that bloom in the meadow*
> *And a handful of forget-me-nots.*

Short as it is, the poem is filled with Anne Frank's gentleness and her sensitivity to beauty. The open book shows pictures of flower baskets on each page. From the flower basket on the left, a dove takes flight with a letter in its bill.

Two months after this poem was written, Holland, where the Franks had taken refuge, was invaded and occupied by German troops. As Nazi persecution of Jews intensified, Anne, with other members of her family, was forced to live confined in the attic of a building in Amsterdam. Here they remained for two years until they were discovered and arrested by the Gestapo. Anne was sent to a concentration camp where she died in 1945, just days before the liberation of the camp by British forces. She was only 15.

THE POISON OF LIES

The Nazis murdered six million people—simply because they were Jews. They ripped babies from their mothers' arms and flung them to their deaths; they used children as guinea pigs in appalling medical "experiments"; they herded people into gas chambers; guards shot prisoners just to "let off steam." The Nazis spread false rumors about the Jews, the victims of their atrocities, denouncing them as brutal and inhumane, morally corrupt, the dregs of humanity. Everything that was most true of the Nazis themselves, they ascribed to the Jews.

These lies, repeated again and again, acted like poison that, drop by drop, penetrated the hearts and minds of the German people, paralyzing their senses. Eventually, people were so transformed that they accepted without question the most evil of deeds.

"Forget-me-not." The name of the flower that Anne wished to send her friend was a plea not to be forgotten. But who could forget her? Who can forget the millions who died in the Holocaust?

Rabbi Hier has a personal connection to the Holocaust. Though he was born and raised in the United States, almost all of his relatives in Poland were killed in the Holocaust. Once when he was staying in Vienna he had a chilling experience. As he sat down in the hotel barber's chair, he noticed a signed photograph of Hitler hanging proudly on the wall. It was a terrible shock. This was the late 1970s, and yet Nazism survived there in Vienna.

NOT HATRED OR REVENGE

Rabbi Hier is committed to perpetuating the struggle of Simon Wiesenthal, after whom the Center is named. Himself a survivor of the death camps, Wiesenthal has been dedicated to bringing to justice Nazi war criminals who went into hiding after the war. He has been motivated solely by his duty as a survivor. Justice is his motive, not hatred or revenge.

Wiesenthal's international visibility is very high. His existence is a constant thorn in the side of former Nazis and all who want the past to be forgotten. On several occasions, his life has been threatened. Attempts have been made to implicate him in scandals, and all sorts of plots have been hatched to destroy his credibility. Yet, for over half a century, he has remained faithful to his struggle for justice.

"Without Simon Wiesenthal," writes Rabbi Hier, "the subject of the Holocaust would not really receive serious attention anywhere in the world... There was still a long period of time between 1945 and the early sixties: a crucial period when there was the greatest pressure to forget." Some cynically suggested the reason for that pressure was that dead Jews don't vote, whereas living ex-Nazis do.

The denial was remarkable. Some members of the older generation in Germany and Austria intentionally spread lies about the past, claiming that Anne Frank's diary was a fake and that the "so-called" gas chambers were only for the purpose of disinfecting prisoners' clothing. Their influence was so potent that in 1958, youthful demonstrators interrupted a stage production of *The Diary of Anne Frank* in Linz, Austria, distributing leaflets with the message: "This play is a fraud. Anne Frank never existed. The Jews have invented the whole story because they want to extort more restitution money."

Simon Wiesenthal was living there, and when he heard about the demonstrators, he rushed to the theater to investigate. Later, he wrote of the event: "These young rowdies were not guilty; their parents and teachers were. The older people were trying to poison the minds of the young generation because they wanted to justify their own doubtful past. Many of them were trapped by their heritage of ignorance, hatred and bigotry. They hadn't learned anything from history."

"HE'S DYNAMITE"

Beneath an intelligent and urbane manner, a fierce anger against evil and injustice burns in Rabbi Hier's heart. Whenever he hears anti-Jewish propaganda, he springs immediately to the offensive. He rebuts it, demands an apology, and widely publicizes the truth, using every method at his command to cut off the poisonous weed of hatred at the root. "He's dynamite," says Wiesenthal of Hier. "The man is never quiet. He is always trying to do things no one else has ever tried." He lectures, he writes, he appears on televised debates and he meets with political leaders across the globe.

He motivated the U.S. Senate to hold public hearings, sounding the alarm about the threat posed by neo-Nazi groups. He doesn't allow the smallest slur to go unchecked, because he never forgets the speed with which a civilized society was transformed into a demonic one.

Wiesenthal's life has been dedicated to the belief that hope lives when people remember. Rabbi Hier's work proclaims: Hope lives as long as we do not remain silent.

The lies about the Holocaust are not unlike the lies still told in Japan, that claim, for example, that the Nanking Massacre, where untold numbers of Chinese were brutally slaughtered, never took place. For the sake of peace, we must never forget the staggering horrors of war.

In the same way that the Nazi regime tried to establish the Aryan "race" as a chosen people, the Japanese militarists called Japan the "land of the gods." The belief that there is a divine or superior people always requires the lie that there are inferior peoples. For the Nazis, they were the Jews and the Gypsies; and for the Japanese military, the Koreans and the Chinese. Those lies resulted in cruel slaughter by the Nazi and Japanese armies.

When we deny that Auschwitz or the Nanking Massacre ever happened, aren't we murdering the victims all over again? Surely seeking to keep our young people in the dark by failing to teach them the truth about history is far more shameful than having to face and come to terms with a shameful past.

WE WILL NOT FORGET

To teach the importance of human rights, Hier established the Wiesenthal Center's Museum of Tolerance. I visited the Museum on January 31, 1993. Rabbi Hier graciously showed me around the facility, even though he was very busy preparing for its official opening early the following month. There were models of Auschwitz and a ghetto where countless Jews were confined and then massacred. The many photographs and audiovisual resources gave voice and identity to their now silent subjects. I felt a powerful sense of outrage welling up within me. How, I wondered, could we ever forget these tragic events? How can we fail to be enraged by them?

Yet just around the time I made my visit, books and weekly tabloids in Japan were touting the idea of an "international Jewish conspiracy"—the same absurd lies that were once spread by the Nazis. The victims of the persecution were being attacked and painted as its perpetrators.

From my meeting with Rabbi Hier emerged the project of bringing the exhibition "The Courage to Remember: Anne Frank and the Holocaust" on a tour of major Japanese cities. This exhibition, a collaborative effort of the Simon Wiesenthal Center, Soka University and the Soka Gakkai, touched the lives of more than one million people. It is my hope that it has helped dispel some of the ignorance about the Holocaust in Japan. In a speech at the exhibition's opening in Hiroshima, Rabbi Hier declared that each individual must have the determination to stand up for truth and justice. He called on people to speak out loudly, clearly and unmistakably for human rights, in every area of the globe where those rights are being violated or threatened.

He also proposed that a series of lectures be held at the Simon Wiesenthal Center to make others aware of the unsung heroes of human rights around the world, to be entitled the "Makiguchi Memorial Human Rights Lecture Series." This choice of title is a tribute to the fact that Tsunesaburo Makiguchi, the founding president of the Soka Gakkai, fought to protect people's fundamental human rights from the oppressive forces of Japanese militarism during World War II, and died in prison for those convictions.

When I was invited to give the first lecture in the series in June 1996, I closed my speech with the following poem:

> *It is my belief—*
> *that a person, a people,*
> *who embrace a noble philosophy,*
> *people upholding sublime faith—*
> *that only a person, a people,*
> *who, amidst raging storms,*
> *live out the drama*
> *of reality and grand ideals,*
> *subjected to and enduring*
> *limitless persecution—*
> *that only such a person,*
> *only such a people,*
> *will be bathed in the sunlight*
> *of perpetual joy, glory and victory.*

In my heart, I called out to the millions in Europe and in Asia who had been trampled beneath lies and violence: I will not forget you! We will never forget. We will fight for the truth to be known.

For when lies are allowed to go unchallenged, they spread like fire. And from that neglect can arise another Hitler.

As Rabbi Hier has said: A world without a past is a world without a future.

FANG ZHAOLING

Paintings of the Heart

FANG ZHAOLING (1914–), PEOPLE'S REPUBLIC OF CHINA

Hong Kong artist and calligrapher Fang Zhaoling studied at Oxford University and the University of Hong Kong before devoting herself to art from the 1950s. Incorporating traditional Chinese painting with modern themes and new techniques, she developed a distinctive and original style. Her paintings are noted for their bold compositions and powerful brushwork, which express empathy for the joys and sorrows of life and a refreshing vision.

FANG ZHAOLING

Paintings of the Heart

❧

I first met Chinese painter and calligrapher Fang Zhaoling in 1996, at a dinner for honorees of the University of Hong Kong. I found her to be an engaging conversationalist, and a woman of great learning and character. We discussed a wide range of subjects, from the cultural history of the Silk Road to current events. She was vibrant and energetic, shining like a jewel. It was only later that I learned that her inner life had been ground and polished to its present brilliance through profound suffering.

Zhaoling's father was one of the first people to build a modern textile factory in China. Born on January 17, 1914, she grew up enjoying the warmth and comforts of a loving, cultured family life.

Her father rented a house to the general of one of the warlords who effectively divided military control of China among them. For their safety, he arranged to have his family live in a separate location. One day, when Zhaoling was 11, her father was coming to get his family by boat, the usual means of transport in the area. It was just around noon. Suddenly, three soldiers who had been lying in wait aimed their guns and started shooting at the boat. The bullets pierced her father's luggage and entered his body. "Get down! Get down!" were his final words to Zhaoling and her sister.

In the wake of her husband's assassination, Zhaoling's mother sought to prepare her daughters for life in a turbulent world by providing them with the finest possible education. It was her conviction that this was the most certain thing she could offer them; that a person who continues to learn has nothing to fear no matter how the times may change. The young Fang Zhaoling was tutored in subjects ranging from the Chinese classics to European history. She also enthusiastically practiced the art of traditional Chinese painting.

THE YEARS OF FLIGHT

In 1931 she went to England to study at the University of Manchester where she was the only female Chinese student. Her husband to be, Fang Yingao, was already studying at Manchester when she arrived. He was the son of a renowned general resisting Japan's aggressive military expansion in China. They married as students; his major was economics and hers was modern European history. Contrary to the prevailing mores of the times, Fang Yingao was broadminded and treated her as an equal. They discussed everything. Their first child, a son, was born. They were happy.

But they could not escape the effects of war. In 1940, the hellish flames of Hitler's aggression were lapping the shores of England. The lights of safety and security were being extinguished. Bombs fell like rain—a rain as dark as the human heart, a rain of sheer hatred.

Seeking refuge, the couple traveled to Norway and then New York. Pregnant, she traveled three days and nights by train to arrive in Los Angeles en route to China. One week after the family's arrival in Shanghai, twin daughters were born.

They made their way to Hong Kong but here again they encountered war. The Japanese army invaded, perpetrating unspeakable atrocities against the local population. The young family, driven by the sound of marching boots and gunshots, traveled from place to place across the vastness of the Chinese mainland. They found temporary refuge in the dreamlike isolation of Guilin, famous for its dramatic landscape of rivers and towering cliffs. They went to Chongqing, the strategic center of Sichuan province. The children born during these years each had a different birthplace.

Each day Fang Zhaoling felt as if she were taking her children by the hand to make another desperate passage over stretches of thinly frozen ice. It was her husband, Fang Yingao, who gave her hope and reminded her of her special talent. Never forget your painting, he encouraged her, that is the path you must pursue. It was thanks to his warm supporting voice that she was able to survive. Just being near him, feeling his broad, embracing spirit, brought courage forth from within her.

ALONE

Even after the invading Japanese army withdrew in defeat, the flames of civil war continued to rage. In 1948, after almost ten years of wandering and flight, the Fang family settled in Hong Kong. The following year, the "new China" was born. But tragedy struck once more. On September 9, 1950, just as the family was starting to savor the joys of peace and a return to normal life, Fang Yingao died of illness, apologizing in his final breath for leaving her to raise the children alone.

Stunned, Fang Zhaoling turned her gaze to the heavens. She pondered the cruel mystery of fate. At thirty-six, she was alone with eight children to care for.

The oldest was eleven, the youngest three: six boys and two girls. Eight sets of eyes all shone with the same question, the same fear: "What are we to do? How are we to live from now on?" She held her children tight, trying in vain to hold back her own tears which fell in hot streams down her cheeks.

Her loss made all the more poignant the memories of their times together.

"Looking back, you were always there... you were always kind. We shared everything. Why must death be the one thing we can't share...?"

Waking in the middle of the night, she found herself alone. Alone in a dark maze. In the midst of a stillness in which the stars themselves seemed to have stopped moving. Alone. She felt the burden of an enormous void, as deep as the oceans, as vast as the sky.

Again and again, she reminded herself that she must go on living. And yet…

There is nothing more fragile than the human heart. At the same time, there is nothing more indestructible. She had reached the point that is known only by hearts that have been plunged into the very pit of grief, but have refused to die. It is there that we encounter a light that shines from the depths of life, from the compassionate essence of the universe. Only those who have known the biting cold of winter can truly appreciate the compassion and love of the sun.

LOOKING FORWARD

Even the longest night will eventually give way to dawn. One day, she felt her husband's presence. She could almost hear his voice. She did, in fact, hear him speaking within her heart, offering the same warm encouragement he always did. "I am with you, here, now. I will be with you always," he seemed to say.

And it was then that Fang Zhaoling vowed never again to dwell on the past. She realized that to do so was to make her husband a part of the past, a time that was gone, never to return. If I move forward, she thought, he will advance alongside me, with me. We will be together.

Among her favorite phrases is this passage from the *I Ching* (Book of Changes): "Heaven is powerful and untiring. Thus the superior man ceaselessly strengthens himself." To "strengthen yourself" means to encourage yourself, to advance without cease, just like the sun. As she expresses it: "The Earth spins on its axis each day, it never stops. If people live like the Earth, energetically pursuing their chosen work, they will enjoy health and develop the spiritual aspects of their life."

Embracing the precious treasure of a bundle of her husband's letters, Fang Zhaoling began a new life. She started running the small trading company her husband had left her. She began giving classes in painting. She made efforts to ensure that, just as her mother had before her, she would give her own children the best education possible.

In the children's voices she heard her husband's voice; in their actions she saw him. As the children grew, he grew also, becoming an ever-larger presence in her heart.

When she had achieved a degree of financial security, Fang Zhaoling set out once more on the path of learning. While intensively studying calligraphy and painting, she enrolled in the University of Hong Kong. She followed this with studies at Oxford University. She took up residence in London, where she studied oil painting and other elements of the Western art tradition.

She sought out new frontiers in Chinese painting. She was determined to develop an entirely new and unique way of portraying human figures and landscapes. Drawing from the masters of past and present, East and West, she wanted to express and create forms that were hers and hers alone. She once told me that she felt it took her 50 years to develop her own style of painting.

Victory, whether in art or in life, is found in dedicated, uncompromising effort. She traveled to Germany, the United States, Brazil, constantly studying and exhibiting. She missed her children, and it was hard being away from them, but from her example of earnest effort they learned the most precious lessons of all. They now say that they cannot remember seeing her go a whole day without taking up her brush.

A SKILLED PAINTER

Buddhism teaches that the heart is like a skilled painter. Both art and our lives are faithful expressions of what is in our hearts. Everything, I believe, comes down to that. As a Chinese classic states: "If the heart is correct and true, so is the brush."

Through all adversity, Fang Zhaoling's heart remained undefeated. She continued always to burn with passion, with the determination to keep fighting. She advanced, pushing the limits of endurance, determined to accomplish something each day, to make each day a step forward.

The experience of having endured and overcome such profound sadness has completely liberated her from fear. The sufferings of life have dug out a deeper, wider space for the world of her heart; and paintings of stunning beauty and power have grown in that inner expanse. In everything she sees she feels the light, the shapes and shadows, of life itself. Mountains, rivers, the ceaselessly changing landscapes—all these appear as a vast song of life. With every passing year, a new cosmos comes into being within her.

The human figures in Fang Zhaoling's paintings exude an innocent joy. Her landscapes often feature forbidding cliffs and mountains, but if you look closely, there is always a way through them.

Her children have all grown into fine, accomplished people. One is a simultaneous interpreter for the United Nations; another, a company president; one is a lawyer and two are doctors. One of her daughters, Anson Chan Fang On-Sang, was the first woman, as well as the first Chinese, to serve as chief secretary of the Hong Kong government. She played a crucial role in the return of Hong Kong to China and later became known as the conscience of Hong Kong.

The day after we met, mother and daughter were both conferred with honorary doctorates from the University of Hong Kong—an event that was quite literally the talk of the town.

Later, Fang Zhaoling sent me two family photographs. The first, taken in 1951, one year after the passing of her husband, shows eight sweetly innocent children huddled together. The second, taken in 1995, shows eight men and women, dignified and confident, gathered smiling around their mother. Seeing them, I felt that these two photographs condensed the history of a family. I could not but imagine that Fang Yingao, the children's father, must be watching over them, happily, proudly. Several months after our first meeting, I wrote a poem for Mrs. Fang, in which I attempted to put into words the impression she had made on me:

That day you stood there,
smiling with maternal warmth and refinement.
Like red plum blossoms that bloom
after the bitter winter cold,
you stood serene,
the drama of your turbulent years
enfolded in your heart,
as if proclaiming: "I have triumphed in my life."

Into her eighties, she continued to rise early and paint for six to eight hours each day. Staying busy, she says, is the secret to long life. "If you are engaged and occupied with your work, you don't bother worrying about small problems. You don't dwell on things or let them bother you."

In January 1997, when she was already 83, she inscribed a calligraphy that seems to sum up her life:

Once more I rise
to scale the high peak.

⟞⟝

Martin Seligman

Learning to Hope

MARTIN SELIGMAN (1942–), UNITED STATES

Martin Seligman is known for pioneering work in the promotion of "positive psychology," including the study of positive emotion, positive character traits and positive institutions.

He is Fox Leadership Professor of Psychology in the Department of Psychology at the University of Pennsylvania and a best-selling author on optimism and the creation of happiness. He was president of the American Psychological Association for 1996.

MARTIN SELIGMAN

Learning to Hope

—⁂—

Optimists and pessimists inhabit different worlds, reacting to the same circumstances in completely different ways. Let's say that you ask a friend at work or school to have lunch with you, and they turn you down. How do you react? A pessimist might think, "They don't like me; it's because I'm not interesting or attractive." Such thoughts provoke further gloomy ruminations, gradually leading you to feel that you're worthless. In contrast, a person with an optimistic approach to life might think that their friend is simply busy and plan on trying again another time.

Let's take another example. Before going out for the evening, a woman has asked her husband to bathe the children and put them to bed. Getting home she finds them all sitting together in front of the TV. One reaction might be: "I can't believe it! Why can't he do the simplest thing I ask him to? Why do I always have to be the one who shouts at the children to go to bed? Why do I always have to be the 'heavy'?" Too furious to speak, she angrily snaps off the TV and marches the children off to bed. After a tense period, she starts to regret her anger and to think morosely: "I hate myself when I act this way! But I wish he'd show more understanding! He doesn't really care about me, that's why he acts this way. Our marriage is a failure…" Negative feelings increase like a snowball rolling down a hill.

But there is another way to react to the same situation. It is equally possible, finding them all watching TV together, to say, "My, my, are you still up? Is it such an interesting program? Well, then, let me watch a little with you. But you have to go to bed soon." Someone who reacts this way might think, "Today he wanted to spend some time with the kids," let go of their initial anger and adopt a positive attitude.

PESSIMISTIC THINKING

Dr. Martin Seligman, former president of the American Psychological Association, identifies three characteristics of pessimistic thinking. He describes these in his fascinating book *Learned Optimism: How to Change Your Mind and Your Life.*

The first is permanence. This means regarding temporary, passing events as lasting and unchanging states. For example, your boss berates you about something. You react by thinking, "I really hate her," and you go on from there to think of all the things you don't like about your boss. Your boss's reprimand is a single, passing event, but you turn it into something permanent by thinking, "She's always like that," and "No matter what I do, she'll never change." On the other hand, the optimistic person thinks, "The boss is in a bad mood today. She must have something on her mind," limiting the event to that day and not extending it any further.

The second characteristic is pervasiveness. When one thing goes wrong, a pessimist thinks that everything is bad. This is like thinking that you can't handle any school subject just because math is hard for you. When someone points out a mistake to a person with this attitude, they think, "I'm no good. I can't do anything," and become dejected. Instead of simply thinking that here is something that has to be fixed, individuals like this think that their very worth as a person has been denied. A single spot grows into a huge black cloud filling their mind. They lose confidence and make more mistakes, creating a downward cycle.

The third characteristic of pessimism is personalization. That is, thinking that anything bad that happens is your fault and anything good must be credited to other people or to chance. For example, when an optimistic athlete or team loses a game, they think, "You win some, you lose some" or "The other team was really on top of their game today." They don't simply blame the loss on themselves. But when a pessimistic athlete loses, they think, "I've lost my concentration, I let so many good ones go by," or "With hitting like that, we'll never win." When two teams are of the same level in ability, explains Dr. Seligman, the optimistic team is more likely to win.

Of course, we can't lose sight of reality and, in an extreme version of optimism, cheerfully blame everything bad that happens on others. However, pessimism causes us to criticize ourselves needlessly.

THE POWER OF THE MIND

When I met with Dr. Seligman during his visit to Japan in 1997, I expressed my sympathy with his views. The mind, I noted, is a wondrous thing. As Milton wrote in *Paradise Lost*, "The mind is its own place, and in itself / Can make a Heav'n of Hell, a Hell of Heav'n." Buddhism teaches that the quality of our lives ultimately depends upon our state of mind. Buddhism is a psychology of hope, and hope is my favorite word.

Nodding in agreement, Dr. Seligman leaned his large frame toward me and spoke in a deep, mellow tone: "Optimism is hope. It is not the absence of suffering. It is not always being happy and fulfilled. It is the conviction that though one may fail or have a painful experience somewhere, some-time, one can take action to change things."

According to Dr. Seligman, optimistic people are more likely to succeed at work and in personal relationships. They are healthier and live longer. He notes that the impact of our attitude on health becomes more pronounced from the mid-forties on.

Dr. Seligman's theories are based on the idea that people can change. By changing our way of thinking, we can change our lives.

During our discussion, Dr. Seligman commented that psychology after World War II was mostly concerned with those who had profound psychological problems. He explained, however, that he aspired for what he called a "positive psychology"—one that gives ordinary people courage, hope and strength.

Dr. Seligman confesses that he himself was a pessimist by nature; he had to learn to be optimistic. It was his father's death, he says, that led him in this direction. His father, a talented civil servant, decided to run for high public office in the state of New York. Around that time, when Dr. Seligman was only 13, his father suffered a series of debilitating strokes that left him paralyzed. His father lost all hope and plunged into a terrible sense of helplessness. He remained in that state until his death several years later. Seeing this, Dr. Seligman says he decided to investigate what it is that makes people feel powerless over their circumstances, and to inquire as to whether there might be some way to overcome these feelings.

Perhaps because he was originally motivated by these sad events, Dr. Seligman's scholarship is imbued with a warm humanity, the noble aim of helping others. Dr. Seligman's "psychological revolution," based on a deep confidence in the positive potential of human beings, has been called by some the most important development in psychology since Freud.

HABITUAL THINKING

Dr. Seligman emphasizes the need to become aware of the explanations we make for events, the unconscious dialogue we conduct within ourselves when we run up against some kind of problem. We tend not to notice the quirks in our own thinking because over the years they have become habitual.

One method Dr. Seligman suggests for becoming aware of these thought-habits is to write down what we are thinking to ourselves when we encounter some minor frustrating situation. If we find that we tend to react to events pessimistically, we can practice "disputing" our own negative beliefs to overcome that tendency.

For example, let's say you rang and left a message for your friend to call you, but he doesn't return your call. People with pessimistic thought-habits will explain the situation to themselves by saying, "He must be ignoring me" or "Maybe he doesn't call because I'm always selfish." If we heard someone else saying such a thing, we would be quick to point out that they are jumping to negative conclusions. But when the conversation is just between us and ourselves, we seem to be ready to believe the worst. This is why learning to objectively dispute your own negative beliefs can be helpful: "As a matter of fact, he's always been very nice to me. He wouldn't ignore me. He said he was having a busy week."

Or you could try saying to yourself: "Even if he is ignoring me, what about it? I can't be perfect in everything and not everyone is going to like me all the time. Whatever others may think, I'm doing my best. I'm going to give myself credit for trying at least!"

Dr. Seligman says we should practice this kind of optimistic thinking, inscribing optimistic phrases in our minds. Prayer or meditation can be used by people of religious faith to engrain positive habits of mind. Once we have acquired the skill of being optimistic, we never lose it. In that sense, it's a lot like learning to swim or ride a bicycle.

LEARNING THE JOY OF CHALLENGE

Likewise, Dr. Seligman points out, in most cases, poor grades are not an indication of lack of ability; rather, they are an indication that the student tends toward a pessimistic view of her- or himself. Students who believe they are not bright or lack ability give up quickly whenever they encounter a challenge. Convinced they can't do something, they don't even try. It's not that they aren't motivated or able. It's just that they haven't learned the optimism that will help them overcome obstacles.

All it takes is for parents to think that a child is not bright, and the child, sensing this, will adopt a pessimistic self-image. It's even worse if every time the child does poorly on a test the parents say things like: "You never try hard enough," "You're lazy" or "You're so careless that you don't even check your work." Gradually the child, too, will come to see himself as lazy and careless.

When children who have become pessimists trip over a small pebble, they will transform it in their mind into a huge mountain. Terrified of failure, they will now be more apt to fail, because of that very fear.

The best way to help children develop a positive outlook is not to demand that they accomplish this or that, but to reassure them that they can succeed. When they fail at something, instead of scolding them, you can say, "You usually do so much better. This isn't like you." Dr. Seligman is not suggesting that we constantly praise children, but that we teach them to have the confidence to overcome obstacles as well as communicate to them the joy that is to be found in that challenge.

OVERCOMING SELF-CENTEREDNESS

Dr. Seligman notes that while people in the developed world enjoy greater wealth and security than ever before in history, there has been a dramatic upsurge in those who are pessimistic and suffer from depression. He identifies the cause of this epidemic of pessimism as self-centeredness. He also notes the decline of larger institutions of support, such as religion, society as a whole, the ties of extended families and local communities. Education has also contributed, he says, by concentrating too much on not hurting children's self-esteem, while neglecting to teach a way of life in which they do not fear failure, but find joy in overcoming challenges. In other words, adults must conquer their own self-centeredness. Adults must show children the way to surmount obstacles.

One of Dr. Seligman's surveys, incidentally, revealed a very interesting fact: a mother's level of optimism and that of her child are generally quite similar. This was true whether the child was a son or a daughter. In contrast, fathers' impact on children in this regard was much more limited.

Buddhism, I believe, is a psychology of hope, a powerful life-philosophy of hope. A Buddha is one who has complete understanding and mastery of the unfathomable powers of the mind. Changing our state of mind can open the way to infinite realms of positive change. My mentor Josei Toda referred to this process as "human revolution."

Moreover, Buddhist philosophy clearly explains that a profound transformation in the state of mind of a single individual—just one person's "human revolution"—can have a positive influence on an entire society. If our minds have this kind of power to change the world, how could our personal lives be beyond our ability to change and direct toward our highest goals? From this perspective, there is absolutely no reason to give up or feel hopeless.

Rather than phrases like: "It won't make any difference" or "It's impossible," whatever our circumstances, let's learn to say: "I am the happiest person in the world! There has never been a better family than mine!"

DAVID NORTON

Life as an Adventure

DAVID NORTON (1930–95), UNITED STATES

David Norton worked as a uranium prospector and a civil engineer before pursuing his fascination with ethics and philosophy. He then taught philosophy at the University of Delaware for nearly 30 years. The theme of ethical individualism—self-actualization combined with social responsibility—runs through his work, as well as a passionate interest in the kind of education needed to enable the fullest human development and moral integrity.

DAVID NORTON

Life as an Adventure

⌐—⌐

Many people talk about philosophy, but few actually apply it to their life. The late David Norton, professor of philosophy at the University of Delaware, was a person who practiced what he preached and who lived according to his convictions.

On education and the pedagogical theories of Tsunesaburo Makiguchi, the educator who founded the Soka Gakkai in 1930, Dr. Norton's words resonated with great depth:

> Mr. Makiguchi was working with the profound truth that all human beings have an innate desire to learn and to grow. We see this in young children. When they first learn to walk, for example, they take their first steps and their faces light up with joy. And from then on, we can't stop them from walking.

On another occasion, he wrote:

> [Makiguchi] proposed that the aim of education must be the happiness of children.... By "happiness" Makiguchi referred not to pleasure but to the satisfaction of work well done when it is the right work for the individual to do.

Norton keenly experienced this kind of satisfaction when he was still in his teens. When he was 16, he saw smoke jumpers fighting a forest fire in Priest River, Idaho. Smoke jumpers are volunteer fire fighters who para-chute into inaccessible areas and cut trees or dig trenches to keep forest fires from spreading. This is not only physically demanding but also extremely dangerous—not the kind of work that would attract most people. But for the young Norton, who had a desire somehow to help others, the smoke jumpers were profoundly inspiring. The next summer, at the age of 17, he became one himself. Despite the danger, he went ahead. He was convinced that facing one's fear and serving society makes for the highest way of life.

PEAK EXPERIENCE

Norton called smoke jumping a "peak experience." He said that by facing danger and testing his courage he felt a tremendous expansion of his potential. Placing his life on the line had given him the quiet confidence that he could do anything if he tried.

"What Makiguchi recognized," Dr. Norton told me, "is that it is imperative that education should nurture and encourage this innate desire to learn and further help it to grow, rather than stifling or killing it... Unfortunately, in Makiguchi's time, education in Japan crushed that innate desire, as does education in America today."

Norton refrained from criticizing modern Japanese education but, as many have pointed out, Japan's test- and performance-oriented education-al system is very destructive.

In this connection, I would like to share a story about a Japanese ele-mentary school teacher.

One young girl in his class was completely unable to keep up with the other students. She sat at her desk every day, looking down with a dull and joyless expression. At first, the teacher wanted to do something to help her, but after a while he gave up. One of his fellow teachers callously told him: "Human beings are just like fruit; twenty to thirty percent is always worthless, and there's nothing you can do about it." In his heart, the teacher started to wonder if the schoolwork was in fact beyond this girl's innate abilities, as her scores on aptitude tests were extremely low.

Then, during one recess period, he noticed her playing with a puzzle, trying to put plastic pieces together so that they would fit neatly into a box. As he watched her through the window, she seemed to be finding the puzzle quite a struggle.

Just as he was about to offer to help, she fit all the pieces into the box perfectly. She stood up and yelled, "I got it!" her face sparkling with an expression of delight he had never seen before.

The teacher suddenly felt remorse for his previous attitude. How dare he give up on her! Wasn't it his job to make sure that each child could walk out of his classroom with the confidence that they could accomplish anything if they really tried?

He had never really thought about how painful it must be for her to sit in school for six hours a day, not understanding any of the lessons. The teacher himself had been a bright student from his earliest years in school. He had never experienced the panic, embarrassment and despair of being unable to understand what is being taught. He had never known the misery of being so confused that you can't even keep track of what you understand and what you don't.

He discovered that the girl's parents, both graduates of leading universities, were always calling her stupid. The girl told him, "I counted, and I've been called 'stupid' twenty times in a single day."

The teacher resolved to praise her every day, for every little accomplishment. He would keep saying, "Smart girl, clever girl" to wash away the stain of so much criticism from her heart.

After a year of very hard work on everyone's part, the girl was transformed. Proceeding at her own pace, she finally came to experience the joy of learning. The key was her realization that if she made an effort to achieve something, she could indeed accomplish it. Later, she graduated from university, and today she is a pharmacist.

The teacher reflected: "The smallest failure can destroy a child's confidence, and the smallest catalyst can trigger explosive growth. The challenge for the teacher is to believe in each child's potential."

Dr. Norton described the phrase "You will need to know this," so often used by educators when teaching children, as the "deadliest phrase in the world." It does nothing to attract children's interest; it only forces something on them. Rather, we should offer children the joy of learning. We must try to maintain and sustain throughout children's lives the beaming smiles they show us when they first stand up and start to walk.

"CHERRY, PLUM, PEACH..."

Dr. Norton believed that the Soka Gakkai's value-creating movement took up that challenge. He was impressed when he visited the Soka schools. "The eyes of every child are shining," he said. He loved the name "Soka," or value-creation, and he regarded his encounter with the philosophy of Tsunesaburo Makiguchi as one of the most inspiring experiences of his life. And he wore his Soka University pin, given him when he received an honorary doctorate, with deepest pride to the very end.

When we met in Japan in August 1990, Dr. Norton told me: "I have great respect for the phrase 'cherry, plum, peach and apricot.'" This phrase encapsulates the Buddhist view of education and human nature—how, like the cherry, plum, peach and apricot, all human beings have their own distinct way of flowering and bearing fruit, their own way of expressing their individuality.

I replied, "The unique character of each person, country and culture must be respected to the utmost, and ties of friendship must be formed on an equal basis. This is the original spirit of Buddhism. Insistence on uniformity, the arrogance of authority and the desire to suppress and control others go against all that Buddhism teaches, and against the spirit of true education."

The door to happiness can only be opened from within. The goal of Buddhism is to enable every human being to achieve a flowering of his or her inner potential, to cultivate the innate goodness in each of us. Education shares the same objective: the drawing forth of this inner potential.

The young man who had gained confidence by becoming a smoke jumper was convinced that he should live not as others told him to, but according to his own inner aspirations and desires. Dr. Norton's father and grandfather were both engineers; he, too, started out as an engineer, following a course that accorded with his parents' wishes. But he gradually became aware that this was not the life that he truly wanted to live.

At 35, David Norton reached a turning point, quitting his work as an engineer and taking up the study of philosophy. This was another adventure. He became a graduate student at Boston University and obtained his doctorate in philosophy in only two years.

This, too, was the fruit of the courage he had attained as a smoke jumper. He compared the smoke jumpers with the bodhisattva ideal in Buddhism. They were all ordinary people, he said, but by working for the sake of others, they were able to tap into their hidden potential.

HAPPINESS IS THE GOAL

Students were attracted by his character and would bring their personal problems to him. Because he never treated them with condescension, they felt they could talk to him about anything. Just as surely as water does not run uphill, people never reveal their true feelings to those who look down on them. Dr. Norton had perfected the art of placing himself in his students' shoes and seeing things from their perspective.

For Dr. Norton, the study of philosophy was not an abstract intellectual pursuit; rather, he saw it as a means to help people become happy. Education, government, and religion—all exist to promote people's happiness. If they do not do this, Norton argued, what use are they? In this, he was a powerful champion of humanism. He was able to grasp the essence of humanity, as his learning was at one with his character and his own experience of life.

The same was true of Tsunesaburo Makiguchi. He pursued his studies under adverse conditions. He did not graduate from one of the prestigious imperial universities, so crucial for academic recognition in pre-

World War II Japan. Thus, when he first tried to publish his theory of value-creating education, he was attacked for his presumption. A mere elementary school principal proposing a new theory of education! Government officials told him scornfully that he should put aside his research as a hobby to pursue after retirement.

But Makiguchi would not be dissuaded. He was motivated by a deep love and concern for children to develop a type of education that will enable all children to be happy. He declared: "Ten million of our children and students are forced to endure the agonies of cut-throat competition—the difficulty of getting into good schools, the 'examination hell' and the struggle for jobs after graduation. We can't allow that to continue into the next generation."

David Norton noted that those in power fear and hate any movement that encourages people to think, see and decide for themselves. The essence of Makiguchi's educational philosophy was to teach children to develop an independent spirit so that they would never blindly follow the dictates of authority. And it was this that caused those in power to try to silence him—first by driving him from the educational arena and then by imprisoning him, together with Toda, as a "thought criminal" in 1943, when Japan was consumed by the madness of militarism. Makiguchi died in prison in November 1944 from abuse and malnutrition. Toda survived to rebuild the Soka Gakkai in the postwar era.

"I'VE WON"

In July, 1995, at the age of 65, Dr. Norton was suddenly diagnosed with cancer. The disease was already well advanced, and nothing could be done.

His wife Mary relates, "He was afraid that the pain might reduce him, might make him waver from his philosophy, but it didn't. Pain didn't have a chance... He was gracious in his dying."

Mary Norton talked about the way her husband viewed his approaching death. He had told her that people speak of death as being lonely or solitary, but that he didn't feel that way at all. He said he felt he was surrounded by all his friends—I was touched that he mentioned me as well—and by the people who had inspired him: Thoreau, Emerson, Socrates and Plato, so there was nothing lonely about dying. She said that her husband had faced death without fear and regarded it simply as "another adventure." "I think," she said, "that it was the same kind of test as facing a forest fire."

"I guess the first thing about an adventure," Mary said, "is that it's an opportunity to challenge yourself. It's getting yourself out of situations that are comfortable, where you know what goes, and where you don't have to worry. It's an opportunity to grow. It's really an opportunity to become what you need to be... But, it's one that you must face without fear." This was the spirit with which her husband lived his life.

One of his friends said to him during his illness, "Fight this, Dave, and you can win," but Norton smiled and said, "I already have."

MY REMINISCENCES
Teachers of My Childhood

TEACHERS OF MY CHILDHOOD

The author reflects on his early school experience in the midst of Japan's rising tide of nationalism during the 1930s, and on the teachers whose care and humanity helped nurture his growth.

MY REMINISCENCES
Teachers of My Childhood

W̶hen spring arrives, heaven and earth, towns and cities—everything—takes on a new brightness. The fresh faces of the students just starting school as the cherry blossoms burst into bloom are also bright and shining.

Although many people delight in the beautiful blossoms, few bother to consider the roots that make that blossoming possible. In life, our roots are largely formed by our first experience of education, the years we spend in elementary school.

"Blooming, blooming, the cherry trees are blooming…" I remember my very first school textbook when I entered elementary school in the spring of 1934. Opening it with excitement, I saw a beautiful spring scene of cherry trees in bloom. In the distance there were mountains, and in the foreground the lovely pink cherry blossoms. This Elementary School Reader was the first textbook in Japan to be printed in color; it had just come into use the year before I started school.

"Blooming, blooming"—our teacher wrote the words in big letters on the blackboard. Miss Tejima was tall and slim. Many people, I would imagine, retain a clear memory of their elementary school teachers. I, too, recall Miss Tejima with great clarity—the color of her clothing, her hairstyle, and even her characteristic gestures. On one occasion, Miss Tejima selected me and just one other student from our entire school year and praised our compositions, saying that they were very well written. I was a little embarrassed to be singled out, but I was also very pleased. Everyone is happy when praised sincerely. It builds confidence. Indeed, Miss Tejima's praise may well have influenced my desire to become a writer.

CHANGING TIMES

I attended Haneda Elementary School No. 2 in Tokyo, which at the time was a two-story wooden building surrounded by rice paddies. On frosty winter days, the water in the paddies sometimes froze. On such days, a rowdy band of children, we would stray off the road and, shouting "This way! This way!" cut through the paddies on our way to school. It was a tranquil, idyllic time.

But things were changing quickly. Japan was entering a dark, oppressive period in its history. The Manchurian Incident, which began Japan's invasion of China, took place when I was three. When I was four, there was an abortive coup d'état in which the prime minister was assassinated, and when I was five, Japan withdrew from the League of Nations. Young as we were, we didn't understand what was going on in the world, but the rising waves of the troubled times reached even into our classrooms. A few pages after the blooming cherries in our reader was a page with the barking command: "Advance! Advance! Soldier, advance!"

Another spring came around, and once more the season of cherry blossoms arrived. About this time, my father suffered an attack of debilitating rheumatism and became bedridden. We were forced to scale back our family business of seaweed processing; our lives grew harder day by day. My eldest brother had enjoyed good grades, but he was forced to quit school and go to work to contribute to the family finances.

In the third and fourth grades, I had my first male teacher, Mr. Takeuchi. He had just graduated from teachers college and was young and energetic. He placed a particularly heavy emphasis on physical education: "You can be as smart as you like, but if you don't build a strong body when you're young, you'll be of no use to anyone as an adult. Health is important. Study is important. True education combines both." This appears to have been his credo as a teacher.

I was on the short side and not very strong, so it was no easy thing to meet Mr. Takeuchi's expectations. To this day, I am moved whenever I remember how keenly he encouraged me to develop my physical strength and become healthy. I also remember how he taught us about the meaning of the Olympics, explaining in detail how they were conducted. That was in 1936, the year the Berlin Olympics were held in Germany. Mr. Takeuchi stressed the importance of holding the Olympics on a grand scale every four years as a means of promoting world peace.

He clearly hated war. In the depths of his heart I think that he strongly opposed the militaristic trend of the times, believing in the importance of peace and encouraging children to grow into fine individuals with a true love of peace.

WATCHING OVER GROWTH

In Japan, people who tend and care for cherry trees are called *sakuramori*, a word that implies a sense of careful stewardship. The *sakuramori* look after the cherry trees, encouraging them to grow, tending to their welfare and generally caring for them throughout the four seasons. The care they extend expresses faith in the power of life as it grows and develops into the future. They don't fuss too much about the trees but at the same time they never ignore them. They observe the trees' growth in great detail but allow them to develop freely. For example, if we stake a tree from the very beginning, the tree will rely on the stakes for support and not grow strong on its own.

The roots are especially important. One expert on trees says that the spread of the crown of a cherry tree is mirrored almost exactly by the spread of its roots below ground. If we water the tree only around the base of the trunk, the tree will become "lazy" and not bother to spread its roots far in search of water.

For people, "roots" correspond to the tenacity of our spirit, our refusal to give up. Once a tree has taken firm root, it can survive even on a rocky mountain face buffeted by powerful winds.

Trees are living things. They are not machines. Every cherry tree is unique. They each grow and thrive in different environments. That is why there is no manual that can tell us how to grow a cherry tree. The only way to succeed is to learn the particular tree's character and idiosyncrasies and, taking them into account, warmly care for it.

Each child is also unique. Each has a distinct way of flowering that is his or hers alone. To raise a tree or to foster people, we need a patient faith in their potential to flourish. A child who has poor grades or who is out of control and behaving badly now may in the future grow into a person who does truly remarkable things. It is not at all rare for a child we think we know very well to suddenly change and show us a side we never would have imagined. To the precise degree that we care for and have faith in children, they will extend and spread their roots. And it is this that will give them the strength to survive and make their way successfully through life.

Protection, as in "protection of the natural environment," assumes that nature is frail and therefore needs our protection. But stewardship expresses a spirit of awe and respect for the potential for limitless growth. I believe that such awe and respect for children should be the foundation of education.

VIVID MEMORIES

My teacher in the fifth and sixth grades was Mr. Hiyama. I think he was about 25 or 26 at the time. His broad forehead and clear, bright eyes gave an impression of intellect and acuity. His classes were sometimes challenging, but they were always interesting. Between classes he would read Eiji Yoshikawa's samurai tale *Musashi* to us, gesturing and posing and reading with dramatic expression, bringing the story alive. We were pulled entirely into the world portrayed in the novel; we could see Musashi dashing about and rival swordsman Kojiro brandishing his sword right before our eyes. It took a year, but Mr. Hiyama read the novel to us in its entirety.

During one class, he spread out a large world map before us and asked us where we wanted to go. I pointed to the middle of the vast expanse of Asia. "I see!" he said. "You have pointed to Dunhuang. There are many wonderful treasures there." From that moment a fascination with Dunhuang—the oasis city on the silk trade routes famous for its temples and painted grottos—took hold in my mind.

I may have pointed to China because my eldest brother, whom I loved and respected, had been sent there as a soldier. He was drafted when I was a fourth grader. After him, my next two older brothers were called up for military service.

My father's rheumatism was improving, but with my three brothers away we were short of help and our family finances got worse and worse. When I was a fifth grader, we had to sell our house and move to a smaller one in the same area. The original house had a large yard with a big pond and a tall cherry tree. Whenever I looked up from beneath the cherry tree in our yard, it seemed as if countless bell-shaped flowers were falling from the bright blue spring sky. It was hard to say goodbye to that big tree, but I was glad that I didn't have to change schools because of the move.

A TEACHER'S KINDNESS

Hoping to do what I could to help my family, I got a job delivering newspapers. I woke up each morning while it was still dark and helped out with the seaweed production. When I finished, I delivered my papers and then went to school. After returning from school, I helped with the family business again, pulling the dried sheets of *nori* seaweed off the racks. Then I delivered the evening paper. At night there was the work of cleaning the seaweed, removing any impurities. I look back now on those busy days with fondness.

When I was in sixth grade, we took a school trip to Kansai. We were away for four nights and five days. It was my first trip away from home, and I was very excited. My mother had given me some pocket money, which she had somehow managed to scrape together. I used it to treat my friends, and at the end of the first day it was almost gone. Mr. Hiyama must have been watching me the whole time, because he called to me as I was going up the stairs of the inn where we were staying and said, "Daisaku, your elder brothers are all away at the war. You have to buy your parents a souvenir from your trip."

I was crushed; of course he was right. My mother's face appeared before my eyes. Smiling, Mr. Hiyama called me downstairs. He placed some money in my palm and closed my fingers around it. I think it was two one-yen bills. At that time, it was a large amount of money. I was happy. I breathed a sigh of relief. When I returned home and gave my mother her gift, I told her what had happened. "You must never forget Mr. Hiyama," she said with a gentle smile.

I don't feel that he was giving me special treatment. He wouldn't have been as well loved as he was by so many students if he was the kind of teacher who had favorites. He cared for us all equally, looking deep into our hearts, aware of the family situations that were the "soil" that nourished us. I will never forget the warm affection with which he looked at each of us during our graduation ceremony, large tears running down his cheeks.

In 1940, I graduated from elementary school and entered Haneda Higher Elementary School. My teacher for the next two years was Mr. Okabe, whom we called "Mr. Buccaneer."

He was from Okayama in the western part of Japan and used to make us laugh by telling us that in a past life he must have been the leader of a pirate crew sailing the Inland Sea, which was near his hometown. He was tall with jet-black hair and a handsome, intelligent face. There were some 40 boys in our class—no girls. Mr. Okabe often encouraged me to exercise to strengthen myself physically. He loved sumo wrestling, and taught us various sumo techniques. Even though I was small, I did my best. In summer, we would take off our shirts and run to the Tama River to swim.

At first glance, Mr. Okabe appeared very intimidating, but I never felt afraid of him. It may have been because I was rather shy, but I can't remember him ever scolding me. Once one of the students in our class was hit by another teacher. When Mr. Okabe heard about it he charged into the staff room shouting, "Which one of you hit one of my students?!" He had a very strong sense of right and wrong. He may have seemed gruff on the outside, but we all felt his concern and affection.

GROWING NATIONALISM

When I was in my second year at Haneda Higher Elementary School, its name was changed to Haginaka National People's School. This was mandated by the National People's School Order, a law filled with militaristic overtones that sought to turn children into soldiers. Terms such as "loyal subjects of the Emperor," "drilling" and "group training" became staples of school life, and the gymnasiums of many schools were converted into martial arts training halls. Japan was sliding down the slope from war with China into the even more disastrous Pacific War. In their arrogance and stupidity, the leaders of the day had no thought for the welfare of ordinary citizens. They were driving the nation into the abyss of war with a mix of threats and well-crafted slogans.

Life became harder with each passing day, and cherry trees, whose wood burned well, were cut down one after another for fuel. The tree in our old garden that I loved so dearly was cut down, and a factory for military supplies was built where it had stood.

Education has a truly astonishing power to cast a spell over the innocent hearts of children. Many of the students in my class at the new "national people's school" applied to enlist as soldiers or as civilian colonists on the Chinese mainland. They did this because it seemed to be the highest expression of patriotism: to be a pioneering hero of the new era. I, too, wanted to become a student pilot in the navy after I graduated. Although I was concerned about my family and how they would fare without me, I secretly sent in an application.

"THAT'S ENOUGH!"

I wasn't there when a representative of the navy visited my home. My father sent the man away saying: "My three eldest sons are all in the army. The fourth will be going soon. Do you really plan to take away my fifth as well? No more. That's enough!"

When I got home, my father berated me fiercely. I was never so harshly scolded before or after. It gave me a glimpse of my father's true feelings, which he usually kept to himself.

After graduating, I went to work at the Niigata Steelworks. The war situation had worsened and there was an intensifying sense of impending defeat. In 1945, the last year of the war, air raids on Tokyo started on New Year's Day. Our days were filled with war and air raids. Even so, when spring arrived, those cherry trees that remained began blossoming, honest and true to their nature as always.

On the night of April 15, when the cherry petals were starting to fall, southern Tokyo was attacked in a massive air raid. The anguished sound of the air-raid sirens wailed and mighty B-29s appeared like majestic conquerors, flying steady and low across the sky. The staccato of the strafing from the American planes combined with people's screams. Incendiary bombs fell like a heavy rain. Tongues of flame leapt up here and there, burning madly. In an instant, the entire area was a sea of raging fire, and everyone was desperately trying to flee the conflagration. Parents were separated from small children. Sons and daughters struggled in vain to save elderly parents. All those caught up in this hellish nightmare of death and destruction were filled with searing anguish. Even now, it brings unendurable pain to write of that night.

When the sun rose the next morning, the entire area where I lived had been burned to the ground. Except for Haneda Airport, the town had been reduced to ashes. Both my beloved elementary school and the so-called national people's school had been razed.

Around this time I found myself walking alone, lost in thought. The war dragged on. What would happen to Japan? What would become of my family? How would I live my life? I could not envision a future. Eventually, I found myself in a small section of town that hadn't burned. A little group of cherry trees was in fragrant bloom. It was like a quiet and peaceful dream. In the vast expanse of burnt-out gray, the beautiful colors of the cherry trees glowed like a torch. In the midst of so much death, here was the light of shining life. "Blooming, blooming, the cherry trees are blooming..."

WORDS ON A WALL

In those days, even cherry trees were made into symbols of death. The Japanese people were told to be like cherry blossoms, to scatter courageously in the wind without a whisper of regret. But the cherry trees before me clearly rejected such perversion and spoke to me—powerfully, sublimely—of life. They were overflowing with hope.

"Live! Live fully and deeply! Never cease living! Outlive the winter and let your own unique nature bloom," they said to me. Powerful emotions welled up and filled my heart. On the wall of a burnt-out factory building I used a piece of chalk to write a passage from a poem that I composed. Many people carried chalk with them in those days so that in an emergency they could leave a message that would enable their families to find them. I didn't bother signing my poem, but later I saw that others who shared my feelings had written their thoughts below mine on the wall.

A certain poet once wrote: "Blossoms that scatter, blossoms that remain. Even these will scatter." I had not scattered but had survived, and was now 17. The war had for too long kept me from school and learning. I was filled with the desire to study, to learn, to read books.

I have never forgotten the beloved teachers of my youth. I have stayed in touch with a number of them to this day. Mr. Okabe once wrote to me, exhorting me to live strongly and tenaciously in the face of all obstacles.

In another letter he encouraged me, saying: "The taller a tree grows, the harder the wind blows against it; please endure the wind and snow."

I was able to have a reunion with Mr. Hiyama in Tochigi in 1973. He and his wife had traveled an hour and a half by bus to see me. I hadn't seen him for more than 30 years, but he still had the aura of a great educator who had made a fine job of raising many children. "You don't seem to have any time to rest," he said. "Please be careful not to harm your health." His gaze was just as warm and caring as it had been on that school trip long ago.

Sitting in front of him, I felt as if I had returned to my elementary school days. To a student, your teacher is always your teacher, and to a teacher, your students are always your students. How wonderful it is to have a true teacher! It is easy to encounter a teacher who imparts knowledge, but hard to encounter one who teaches you how to live.

Elementary education is the most critical. But how should we teach elementary school students? It is a very difficult job. That is precisely why I have such tremendous respect for elementary school teachers who do succeed in this challenging work. Are high school teachers more important than elementary school teachers? Are university professors more important than high school teachers? Absolutely not. It is just this kind of erroneous thinking that afflicts our society today: theorists often have the mistaken idea that they are better than practitioners.

FOSTERING THE FUTURE

An architect who theorizes about architecture is in no way superior to a carpenter who can actually build a house. An agricultural expert is not more productive than a farmer who actually grows vegetables or rice. I sometimes think there are too many people who theorize about things and far too few who actually make painstaking efforts to achieve something.

There are many people who love cherries and other flowering trees, but few who truly appreciate the efforts of those who work behind the scenes to keep the trees alive and healthy. The life of an educator is also far from glamorous. Teaching is inconspicuous work that doesn't get much attention; it's a matter of continuous hard work and effort. But it is precisely because of such teachers dedicated to fostering the future that the next generation of children can grow up straight and strong. We must never forget this crucially important fact.

In those dark days, when the power of ultranationalist authorities pressed down so heavily on Japanese society, my teachers held up for their students the great light of humanity. Just like teachers today who are earnestly committed to their profession, they firmly embraced their students and shared their lives with them, while struggling against the intrusions of political power into the realm of education.

If being blessed with good teachers is one of life's joys, there can be no one happier than I.

CORNELL CAPA

Capturing the Eternal Moment

CORNELL CAPA (1918–), UNITED STATES

*Born in Budapest, Cornell Capa, the younger brother of the cele-
brated Robert Capa, is himself an acclaimed photographer who uses
his skills to confront and draw attention to a broad range of social
issues. He coined the phrase "concerned photographer" to define "a
photographer who is passionately dedicated to doing work that will
contribute to the understanding or the well-being of humanity."*

*These concerns are expressed through the activities of the
International Center of Photography, which he founded in 1974.*

CORNELL CAPA

Capturing the Eternal Moment

⟶⟵

"That moment changed my life: the moment I learned of my brother Robert's death." I will never forget Cornell Capa's face as he spoke these words.

Robert Capa had built a reputation as the world's greatest war photographer. During the 1930s and 40s, a period of catastrophic international conflicts, he was always at the front line where the fighting was at its most intense—whether during the Spanish Civil War, the Japanese invasion of China, or World War II. He was bold. He once joked that a war photographer, unless he risked getting his head shot off, couldn't get good pictures. It was his dictum that "if your pictures aren't good enough, you're not close enough."

Cornell Capa, also a renowned photographer, explains that Robert used a wide-angle lens, meaning that he had to get extremely close to take the powerful photos he wanted. "This required tremendous courage, but that demonstrates the kind of man he was." He was dedicated to telling the world the truth, and to do so, he had to risk his life.

Robert's lens captured the grim drama of a soldier falling in a hail of bullets, the wounded groaning in pain, civilians fleeing in panic, the despair carved deep into the faces of small children. This is war, said his photographs: this is what it is really like.

Though he himself had a great love of life, in his role as a photojournalist he faced the gravest dangers. There are times when the freedom to report the truth must be seized in battle and purchased with one's life.

PICTURES OF VICTORY

In October 1990, together with Cornell Capa, I viewed a photo exhibit in Tokyo featuring the works of the Capa brothers. One of Robert's photos was of German farmers whose fields had been burned in an Allied attack. Both as a Jew and as a human being who believed in freedom and liberty, Robert Capa had despised fascism to the very core of his being. His uncle's family and his friends in Hungary, the land of his birth, had been murdered in Nazi concentration camps.

However, in spite of that personal suffering, Robert's vision could transcend the categories of friend and enemy to focus on the suffering of the German people.

I remarked to Cornell Capa that his brother's photographs—starkly capturing the tragedy, pathos, pain and wretchedness of war—were a far more effective indictment of its evil than any war crimes trial. The testimony of his photographs is worth more than any number of words, as he always focused an empathetic gaze on those who were suffering the most.

In October 1943, he joined the Allied troops as they advanced into Italy to liberate Naples, which the Nazis had destroyed before withdrawing. Capa's heart was torn by the sight of the bodies of 20 young boys lying in coffins in a schoolhouse. In the last days of the German occupation, these high school boys had stolen guns and ammunition and fought against the German troops. The coffins were too small for the boys and their bare feet protruded from the open ends. Capa lifted his hat and saluted them, and then turned his camera on their weeping mothers dressed in black.

Later, he was asked to take a victory photo of the generals. However, he subsequently wrote that his photos of those grief-stricken mothers, and not the generals, were the "truest pictures of victory."

World War II came to an end, and Robert Capa joked about having business cards printed that read:

ROBERT CAPA

War Photographer

Unemployed

"And my brother," says Cornell, "told me that he hoped he'd stay unemployed for the rest of his life."

A world without war: In the hopes that such a dream would come true, Robert Capa dashed from battlefield to battlefield, recording its tragic reality.

At age 17, accused of being a communist, he was exiled from Budapest and from that time on, he had no permanent home. His mother, Julia, would become terribly upset each time her beloved son went off to cover another war, and it was always his younger brother Cornell's role to hold her hand and reassure her that Robert would be all right.

Then in 1954, at the age of 40, driven by destiny or by a sense of mission, Robert went to the front lines again, this time to the French Indochina War. His mother was almost hysterical with grief.

On Tuesday, May 25, Robert separated from the French soldiers and was out walking alone in search of better photos. It was three in the afternoon. He stepped off the road into a grassy field, where a land mine was waiting for him.

Cornell recalled for me: "The phone rang. At five to seven in the evening. It was the editor of *LIFE* magazine, who had asked my brother to go to Indochina. He told me that Robert had been killed and that it would be broadcast on the seven o'clock news. He said he wanted to talk to me personally before I saw it aired. I remember that moment as if it were yesterday—no, it is as clear in my mind as if it had just happened."

The US Army regarded Robert Capa as a hero and offered to bury him in Arlington National Cemetery, but his mother refused, saying that her son was "not a soldier, but a man of peace."

"My mother rests beside him, now," continues Cornell. "The word 'Peace' is inscribed on his gravestone."

CARRYING ON THE LEGACY

Robert's death marked a turning point for Cornell Capa. "I made a decision," he says, "to devote my life to preserving my brother's work." He has carried on his brother's legacy of recording the barbaric acts of despots. Cornell established the International Center of Photography and collected and archived the works of his brother and other photographers who championed the cause of peace. At the time, news photographs were regarded as having only transitory value, and no one ever considered preserving them. They had not achieved the recognition they deserve as works of cultural and artistic merit. Cornell has nurtured many young photographers, and through countless exhibitions, lectures and writings, has tirelessly promoted the photographic arts.

He dedicated himself to promoting his brother's work and message throughout the world, setting aside his own career as a photographer. In that decision, I see his greatness as a human being. Robert Capa's fame owes much to the conviction and efforts of his brother.

Cornell had originally intended to become a doctor. However, while studying in Paris, he discovered the world of photography through his brother's influence. "I thought at the time," he relates, "of the impact a photograph can have on people—that it may have the power to heal more hearts than a doctor can." This may be the reason his photographs are filled with such a moving love for humanity. "My mother taught us to love others," Cornell says. "This is the common theme of our work."

Robert's advice to amateur photographers was simple: "Like people, and let them know it." Cornell shares many qualities with his brother: a warmth and charm, an ability to make friends easily, a good sense of humor, an easy-going manner, and a fondness for entertaining those around him. He is a person who loves his friends and is in turn loved by them. It was the same with Robert. And the personal warmth of both brothers comes from their mother. Turning to a selection of Robert's photographs of children, Cornell commented: "Our mother's unsparing love was embodied in Robert's gentle kindness, which he in turn passed on to the children of the world."

THE LENS OF LIFE

Cornell Capa once shared with me the following observation: "Eternity can be distilled in a single moment of life—a moment when a person's humanity, past and future, destiny and life story are revealed with absolute clarity. Photography," he went on, "is the art of capturing that eternal moment and presenting it to others. In that respect, photographers are not simply recorders of events; they are explorers in the earnest pursuit of humanity."

However excellent the camera, photos still need the human aspect. If the photographer's "living lens"—his or her own humanity—is tainted, warped, unfocused or distorted, he or she will not be able to capture the truth of existence in all its myriad forms.

Each moment is unique. It comes, it goes, all in an instant—what Buddhism refers to as a life-moment. Because we know how precious that instant is, we press the shutter. Photography is an art born of a passionate love of life. A person attuned to the extremes of life—people like Robert and Cornell Capa—can perceive the depth of meaning in each passing moment. This gives them the ability to capture the most with the camera of life.

Rosa Parks

Just One Word

ROSA PARKS (1913–), UNITED STATES

Rosa Parks was born in rural Alabama at a time of severe dis-
crimination against African Americans. While working as a seam-
stress, she became active in the Montgomery chapter of the National
Association for the Advancement of Colored People (NAACP).
Her refusal in 1955 to give up her seat on a bus to a white passen-
ger sparked the Montgomery bus boycott. In 1987, she
established the Rosa and Raymond Parks Institute for Self-
Development to inspire and motivate youth.

ROSA PARKS

Just One Word

⟿

There are times when a single word changes history, when an ordinary day takes on an enduring—even eternal—significance. And there are struggles in which a solitary individual becomes a leader who transforms the world. When Rosa Parks refused to obey the order of the bus driver to give her seat to a white passenger and said the single word, "No," the bell of change tolled for the history of African Americans. Many others were involved in the movement that grew out of years of frustration at injustice, but Rosa Parks became a catalyst and a pivot for change.

I first met Mrs. Parks on the Calabasas campus of Soka University of America (SUA) in California on January 30, 1993. I was immediately struck by her warm, motherly personality. This, I thought, must be the gentleness that charms everyone. She was turning 80 and had clearly endured a great deal in her life; yet she had a quiet smile on her lips at all times. She was humble, and yet you could see that she was a person of unbending conviction.

In a survey published in the United States in 1993, in which historians and scholars were asked to name the most influential American women of the 20th century, Rosa Parks ranked number three. The list was topped by first lady and social activist Eleanor Roosevelt.

TIRED OF GIVING IN

Mrs. Parks, a living legend, is widely known as the mother of the Civil Rights movement. Her story is told in school textbooks across the United States and in many other countries around the world. Truly almost no one is ignorant of who she is and what she has done. Yet her extraordinary story demands to be told again.

On December 1, 1955, in Montgomery, Alabama, the 42-year-old Rosa Parks was returning home after a hard day's work in the tailoring section of a department store. After boarding the bus she noticed that the driver was the same unpleasant man who had forced her off a bus on a previous occasion some 12 years earlier. That time the back of the bus had been full, so she had gotten on at the front—and for that, the driver had put her off the bus.

Whites in front, blacks in back: if there weren't enough seats for whites, African Americans had to give up theirs and stand. All types of discrimination designed to make African Americans feel inferior and keep them "in their place" were practiced quite openly at the time. This bus driver hadn't changed in 12 years. "Y'all better make it light on yourselves and let me have those seats," he now threatened. Others stood up, but she remained unmoving.

"I could not see how standing up was going to 'make it light' for me," writes Rosa Parks in her autobiography. "The more we gave in and complied, the worse they treated us."

The tragic history of the blood and tears of millions of her fellow African Americans was behind the determination of this lone woman who refused to move. Their ancestors had been brought to America on slave ships, treated like cattle, and had lived and died amidst immense suffering. Mothers were whipped before their children's eyes, and parents watched in hopeless despair as their children were taken from them and sold. Even after slavery was abolished, African Americans were exploited and lynched and killed with impunity.

"I have experienced many sad events. Many, many," Rosa Parks told me. "One African American youth was arrested on the charge of raping a white woman. He was completely innocent, but he was arrested at the age of 17... and eventually executed at the age of 21."

Rosa Parks had worked with her husband, Raymond, and others to try to save such victims, but they found themselves facing a wall of racial oppression. The civil authorities, the laws, the media and the American people in general all quite blatantly trampled on the inalienable rights of their fellow human beings as if this were perfectly normal and acceptable.

Rosa Parks had had enough of the bullying. As she said, the more she endured, the harsher she was treated.

The bus driver shouted, "Aren't you going to stand up?"

"No."

"Well, I'm going to have you arrested!" he declared.

"You may do that," was Rosa Parks' calm response.

A police officer arrived on the scene. When he asked her why she wouldn't stand up, she asked in return, "Why do you all push us around?"

It has been suggested that Mrs. Parks was simply tired and that is why she remained seated. She is very clear on this point: "The only tired I was, was tired of giving in to discrimination."

WALKING FOR FUTURE GENERATIONS

This incident set off an explosion of anger among the African-American community in Montgomery. This was no doubt largely due to the warm regard in which Rosa Parks was held, as she had long been respected as a cheerful, warm and intelligent woman. A boycott of the bus service was organized, led by the young civil rights activist Martin Luther King, Jr., and others who had long burned with a desire for change. Thousands of African Americans who had previously patronized the buses acted in solidarity. Instead of commuting by bus, they walked or carpooled. Black-owned taxi companies also helped commuters by reducing their fares to those the buses charged. At rush hour, the roads would be lined with people singing as they walked with proud determination. For many, the distance from home to workplace was more than ten miles. But they knew that they were walking the path of freedom, the path of peace.

The story of one participant, related in Martin Luther King, Jr.'s *Stride Toward Freedom* sums up the spirit of the boycott:

> ...Once a pool driver stopped beside an elderly woman who was trudging along with obvious difficulty.
>
> "Jump in, grandmother," he said. "You don't need to walk."
>
> She waved him on. "I'm not walking for myself," she explained. "I'm walking for my children and my grandchildren." And she continued toward home on foot.

Retribution was severe. Rosa Parks was besieged with threatening telephone calls. She lost her job. The newspapers printed false rumors about her, and Dr. King's home was bombed. In the first trial, she was denied the opportunity to testify on her own behalf and was found guilty. But in the face of threats and harassment, Mrs. Parks never thought of fleeing or seeking refuge elsewhere. She was determined to hold her ground, to continue her struggle where she was.

The solidarity of this nonviolent movement remained unshaken; it pricked the conscience of America and the world.

Finally, after a year of appeals and counter appeals, the United States Supreme Court declared segregated busing unconstitutional. From that moment on, the Civil Rights movement gained tremendous momentum, surging forward in a great wave toward equal rights for African Americans.

AN ENCOUNTER

An idea whose time has come is unstoppable. The courage of this lone woman was like a spark that set ablaze a parched field.

Also in *Stride Toward Freedom*, Dr. King described the role played by Rosa Parks in this way:

She was anchored to that seat by the accumulated indignities of days gone by and the boundless aspirations of generations yet unborn. She was a victim of both the forces of history and the forces of destiny. She had been tracked down by the Zeitgeist—the spirit of the time.

I have heard that, prior to my meeting with Mrs. Parks, many of the people around her were naturally wary of Japanese people because of the racist remarks made by a number of our politicians. One can imagine that all sorts of movements might try to exploit her name for their causes, so she has to be very careful. Their concerns seemed to evaporate during her visit to the SUA campus.

She arrived in the midst of the strains of "We Shall Overcome" sung by a welcoming chorus. The moment we met, I felt a spark of recognition pass between us because I, too, have spent my life working for a cause. Mrs. Parks' determination, her tears and her hopes, reverberated in my heart. She also said that she felt she had found a new friend. I shared with her the following passage from a poem of Langston Hughes, a poem which she said had long been one of her favorites.

When I get to be a composer
I'm gonna write me some music about
Daybreak in Alabama ...

And I'm gonna put white hands
And black hands and brown and yellow hands
And red clay earth hands in it
Touching everybody with kind fingers
And touching each other natural as dew
In that dawn of music when I
Get to be a composer
And write about daybreak
In Alabama.

On that occasion, I invited Mrs. Parks to visit Japan, and she gladly accepted, flying to Tokyo in May 1994. This surprised many who know her, since she had never before traveled farther than America's immediate neighbors.

During her visit to Soka University in Japan, she wept as she listened to a student chorus group. She explained that it reminded her of a young Japanese woman, a survivor of the atomic bomb blast in Hiroshima, whom she had once known in the United States. "That young woman liked choral singing, too," she recalled. Listening to the singing of the students, she was unable to hold back her tears. Such is her gentleness and sensitivity, for she always cherishes the feelings of others.

Mrs. Parks related that it was her mother who raised her to be so strong: "My mother taught me self-respect. She always insisted, 'There's no law that says people have to suffer.'"

If we look across the vast landscape of history, the life of one person may seem small and insignificant. Yet, while human beings may appear to be swept up in the torrent of events, it is also clearly human beings who create history.

As Rosa Parks' life demonstrates, the courageous cry of even a single individual standing up for justice can light a flame in the hearts of thousands and change the course of human history.

JAN ØBERG

The Peace Doctor

JAN ØBERG (1951–), DENMARK

Dr. Øberg is cofounder with his wife, Dr. Christina Spännar, of the Transnational Foundation for Peace and Future Research (TFF), a leading think tank in Sweden committed to peace research, conflict mitigation and education. Former secretary-general of the Danish Peace Foundation, he is also co-initiator of the Danish High School for Peace and the Danish Centre for Conflict Resolution. A prolific author, Dr. Øberg serves as an advisor to several international peace foundations.

JAN ØBERG

The Peace Doctor

⎯⎯⎯⎯⎯

Scandinavian peace researcher Jan Øberg compares the work of preventing and healing conflict to the medical arts. The first, crucial step is to make a correct diagnosis. To do this requires direct knowledge. When I met him in December 1995, he had already traveled to war-torn Yugoslavia more than 20 times, conducting some 1,200 interviews, listening to the voices of ordinary citizens and conveying their message to the world. This, he is firmly convinced, is the only way that peace can be achieved.

It puzzles him that while we would never allow ourselves to be operated on by a surgeon who has not undergone rigorous training, we don't insist on the same from our political leaders. In essence, we allow policymakers, diplomats and political leaders to perform "surgery" on the afflicted parts of our planet, despite the fact that they have received no specialized training in treating or healing conflict. The international community, he says, did many things in response to the crisis in the former Yugoslavia, but their actions remind him of a doctor who, failing to determine the true cause of an ailment, amputates the wrong limb. It is no wonder that the "patient"—the former Yugoslavia—died.

During the war, it is estimated that some 10 million land mines were laid, including ones resembling ice creams or chocolate eggs. One little girl picked up a teddy bear and was killed instantly by the bomb hidden in it. How could anyone deploy such barbarous weapons? Who designed and built them? Who profited from their sale? What can be done to stop such inhumanity? These are the questions that plague Jan Øberg, and which gnaw at my heart also.

THE VOICES OF THE PEOPLE

In order to come up with a correct diagnosis, Dr. Øberg and his team talked with a wide spectrum of people on the ground, from heads of state to refugees. They spoke with mothers who had lost their sons to war; with soldiers, journalists, farmers and clergy; with teachers, civil servants and shop owners. The more they listened to the voices of the people, the clearer it became that the image of the conflict being communicated to the world was incredibly distorted.

Central to this was the fallacy that the conflict in the former Yugoslavia was the result of ancient hatreds among the region's various ethnic groups. One young woman Dr. Øberg's team spoke to in Zagreb said: "Up till just a couple of months ago, I hardly knew who of my friends were Serbs and who were Croats."

Before the outbreak of violence, members of different ethnic groups coexisted peacefully within the same communities and workplaces; intermarriage was not uncommon. But then political figures began inciting nationalistic feelings in their grab for power, stressing ethnic consciousness and dividing the population along ethnic lines. An 11-year-old girl in Sarajevo saw through this ploy:

> Among my girlfriends, among our friends, in our family, there are Serbs and Croats and Muslims. It's a mixed group and I never knew who was a Serb, a Croat, or a Muslim. Now politics has started meddling around. It has put an "S" on Serbs, an "M" on Muslims, and a "C" on Croats, it wants to separate them. ...Why is politics making us unhappy, separating us, when we ourselves know who is good and

who isn't? We mix with the good, not with the bad. And among the good there are Serbs and Croats and Muslims, just as there are among the bad. I simply don't understand it. Of course, I'm "young," and politics are conducted by "grown-ups." But I think we "young" would do it better. We certainly wouldn't have chosen war.

But the adults did choose war. Alik, a 13-year-old refugee, recounts:

The soldiers ordered us out of our house and then burned it down. After that, they took us to the train, where they ordered all the men to lie down on the ground. From the group, they chose the ones they were going to kill. They picked my uncle and a neighbor! Then they machine-gunned them to death.

ORGANIZING CONFLICT

As one journalist observed, ethnic tensions and conflicts do not arise spontaneously; they must be incited, aggravated and organized until they reach the point of outright violence. Then, if an atrocity is committed by the members of one group, this is exploited to excite a general hatred of the entire group, deepening and reinforcing the cycle.

And the very structure of peace negotiations works against reconciliation. Only those who purport to represent a distinct ethnic group—those committed to ethnic nationalism—are invited to the table. Those who wish to live together in peace, without regard to ethnicity, are left unrepresented and without voice.

The former Yugoslavia has been described as a nation with seven borders, six republics, five ethnic groups, four languages, three religions, two alphabets, and one name. Dr. Øberg explained to me that one of the first things you realize when you spend time in a place like the former Yugoslavia is the uselessness of trying to grasp the nature or causes of the conflict through simplistic formulations. What is called "the conflict in the former Yugoslavia" is actually at least 30 different conflicts, he says. The causes and histories of these disputes are extremely complex and intricately interrelated.

But in his view, the violence was neither simply an ethno-religious conflict nor was it the inevitable result of the collapse of communism in that country. Rather, he notes, the world's powerful countries made use of the instabilities sparked by deteriorating economic conditions to assure that the order of the post-Cold War world would be favorable to their own interests. Their involvement greatly compounded the tragedy that unfolded. Although he spoke in a gentle tone, his words were scathing and filled with quiet anger.

Despite the complex nature of the conflict, the media and decision makers have shown a strong tendency to oversimplify. Their most dangerous oversimplification has been to view the conflict in stark, black-and-white terms. Because it adopted this view, the international community, which should have served as a fair and impartial mediator, ended up treating the complex patterns of conflict within the former Yugoslavia as a simple struggle between good and evil. Almost without exception, the Serbs were portrayed as evil, while the other groups were depicted solely as victims. This was the story and image that was given to the world. Once established, any facts that didn't fit this story were discarded, and those that did fit were given widespread coverage.

This only made the prospects for fruitful peace negotiations that much more distant. You cannot conduct impartial mediation, Dr. Øberg points out, while harshly condemning just one side. There can be no peace while your boot is on someone's neck. Oversimplification of the conflict opened the way for military intervention to "punish evil." Put differently, one side was demonized in order to justify the use of military force.

Over 70 years ago, the British diplomat Lord Arthur Ponsonby (1871–1946) wrote about the perennial propaganda claims of wartime leaders in his book *Falsehood in Wartime*. Belgian historian Anne Morelli recently shed new light on Ponsonby's analysis, distilling his findings on wartime propaganda into 10 assertions as follows:

1. We do not want war;

2. The other side is solely responsible for the war;

3. The enemy has the face of the devil;

4. It is a noble cause that we defend and not our own interests;

5. The enemy commits atrocities knowingly; if we make unfortunate mistakes, this is involuntary;

6. The enemy uses unauthorized weapons;

7. We suffer very few losses, while the losses of the enemy are enormous;

8. Artists and intellectuals support our cause;

9. Our cause has a sacred nature;

10. Those who question our statements are traitors.

Lies and prejudices are used to promote war; war engenders further lies and prejudices.

TREATING CONFLICT

Sandra, a 10-year-old girl from Vukovar, recalls: "There are so many people who did not ask for this war, or for the black earth that is now over them. Among them are my friends."

Buddhism teaches that health and illness are inextricably linked aspects of human existence, and that illness itself cannot be avoided or eliminated entirely. In the same way, conflict will always be one aspect of human society. The challenge is to respond effectively to conflicts as they arise. If we can do this, the problem can be transformed into an impetus for creative advance, and we and our societies can become stronger and healthier in the process.

More than 700 years ago, the Japanese Buddhist teacher Nichiren compared the methods for attaining peace to the art of medicine, warning those in power that the wrong treatment would never bring about a good result. "If you try to treat someone's illness without knowing its cause," he declared, "you will only make the person sicker than before." Similarly, Dr. Øberg advocates "conflict medicine" and "conflict doctors" to treat conflict—specialists working for the health of humanity, trying to resolve conflict creatively and prevent it from escalating into violence and war. He offers these guidelines as part of his "prescription" for peace:

- War is a sign of failure. It means that we were unable to deal successfully with the underlying conflict.

- Violence is born from the frustration of not being able to effectively resolve conflict.

- The cowardly and intolerant conclude that armed force is the only option. In contrast, nonviolence is a constructive belief that other options exist.

- You cannot cure the sick by attacking and punishing them; likewise, conflict cannot be resolved through force, which only aggravates the problem and makes finding a viable long-term solution more difficult.

- Violence does something that can never be repaired; killing can never be undone.

THE HUMAN DIMENSION

Dr. Øberg says that when discussing peace, the most frequently overlooked aspect is the human dimension: "It's easy to repair houses and infrastructure; it's easy to throw money around and talk about human rights. But what if people deep down keep on hating each other? Will they ever be happy and at peace with themselves? Will their children? We need to make forgiveness and reconciliation a central objective."

Dr. Øberg, together with his wife Christina Spännar and other peace researchers, has conducted conflict study sessions throughout the former Yugoslavia with people who experienced the horrors of the war. In one such session, he and his colleagues brought together Serbs and Croats, young children as well as adults—members of ethnic groups that had been "mortal enemies." When they arrived at the session, these participants saw only the "enemy"—the people who had killed their parents and abducted their children. The atmosphere was like ice.

However, Dr. Øberg's aim was for the participants to speak to each other, not as representatives of one ethnic group or another, but as individual human beings. He let each person tell his or her own story on the condition that they stick to the facts of their own personal experience and avoid attributing blame. It was their first opportunity to talk face-to-face with "the enemy."

What ultimately came out, in halting speech, was their enormous pain. Talking and listening, they wept. And then they realized that they had all suffered alike; they were all victims of the same tragic errors. Eventually, they moved from weeping together to laughing together. Over time, some even became friends and started working together on projects. Dr. Øberg describes this as "one of the most moving experiences of my life."

"Why not have truth and reconciliation committees operating before war?" he asks. "We could learn to fight against war and violence, not each other."

TORAO KAWASAKI

A Bridge Between Civilizations

TORAO KAWASAKI (1914–77), JAPAN

Kawasaki was a pioneer of Arabic studies in Japan who developed his passion for the cultures of the Arabic-speaking world while working for Japan's Foreign Ministry in Egypt, Lebanon and Iraq before World War II. After the war he worked in the private sector and as a commentator on Middle Eastern affairs, and later as assistant professor at Tokyo University of Foreign Studies and professor of Arabic language and literature at Soka University. In 1963, he compiled the first Japanese-Arabic dictionary.

Torao Kawasaki

A Bridge Between Civilizations

—❧—

"I suppose you'd call it a kind of love affair with humanity. Sometimes he'd bring someone home. After an evening of eating and drinking, I'd ask, 'Who was that?' And he'd shrug, 'Not sure, really.' 'What do you mean, you don't know?' To which, he'd reply, 'I just met him on the train home, and I forgot to ask his name.' What do you say to someone like that, someone who can enjoy a person's company without even knowing their name?"

So reminisced a family member of the late Professor Torao Kawasaki, a pioneer of Arabic studies in Japan.

"He studied in Egypt as a young man. Later, while living in Iraq, he once spoke to the king as he was swimming in a pool," this person went on to recount. "He appeared in the local papers as 'the Japanese who greeted the king.' This was before the war, so the presence of a Japanese person in itself was unusual enough to attract attention."

Professor Kawasaki was exuberant, candid and endearing, and had a booming voice. He loathed pomp and ceremony, and was in many ways larger than life. He was bold and energetic yet painstakingly gentle. He was the kind of professor who would call out to any student he encountered, "Hi, there! How are you?"

His roundish figure brimmed with an ardent concern for people. And if he happened upon someone in anguish, someone being mistreated, that vast vat of compassion within him would flare up like a flame.

Kawasaki was in Indonesia when World War II ended. While he could have been repatriated to Japan, he chose instead to stay for more than two additional years. He stayed because he took it upon himself to form a legal team to defend those charged as Class-B and -C war criminals. As one ship after another departed for Japan, he worked frantically to assure his fellow soldiers received justice. He yearned to go home, of course, where his wife and young child were anxiously waiting.

Yet he thought to himself, "How could I abandon my comrades and return to Japan knowing they cannot?"

Committed to doing the right thing, he was a man of deep personal loyalty, free of any hint of calculation.

"I want to compile an Arabic dictionary," Professor Kawasaki once told me. "You still can't find one in Japan to this day! How are we ever going to understand the Arab culture? There are so many dictionaries for the English, German or French languages, it's clearly an unbalanced situation.

"The Arab world encompasses a vast portion of the globe. It's made up of hundreds of millions of people. What are their thoughts, what feelings do they have as they go about their lives? If we have absolutely no idea …then I'd have to say Japan's 'map of the world' is seriously distorted."

"Exactly," I said. "I fully share your concern. It is tragic for different peoples to remain ignorant of each other—unless this changes, peace can never be achieved."

We shared these words on January 27, 1962, two days before I was to leave on my first trip to the Middle East. At the time, there were few people with detailed knowledge of the region and, having heard of Professor Kawasaki through others, I sought his advice on various matters. He taught at the Tokyo University of Foreign Studies while working as a coordinator for the Arabian Oil Co., Ltd.

"Professor Kawasaki, please complete your Arabic dictionary," I urged. "This will be an enormous contribution. It really is the kind of project that the government should undertake."

JAPAN'S FIRST ARABIC DICTIONARY

"That's kind of you to say so," he replied. "To tell you the truth, I haven't been making much progress. Every publisher I approach won't even bother looking into it, saying that the book won't sell. And no printer has access to Arabic type. I suppose they ought to make the type, but everywhere I go, I'm told they could never expect a return from it. I know it's important to turn a profit, but I think there's more to culture than money."

Professor Kawasaki would go on to put the dictionary together himself. Without movable type for the Arabic script, he developed his own method of "photo composition."

He first secured a large volume of textbooks from elementary schools in various Arab countries. He would print Japanese entries such as "to serve" or "has value" on the left side of a page. He would then find their equivalents in the Arabic texts, pasting them on the right column, aligned with the Japanese terms. The handcrafted effort was burdensome and exhausting in the extreme. He would finish his work for the day and then devote his evenings to his dictionary, laboring deep into the night. His family would also pitch in and help.

Professor Kawasaki paid for the publication costs himself. He apparently invested enough to build a house. He had to ask his wife's parents for funding as well.

Finally, Japan's first Arabic dictionary was completed. It was published the year after we met. He went on to complete two other texts, An Introduction to Arabic and the New Japanese-Arabic Dictionary; taken together, they form a trilogy that will forever shine in the annals of Arabic studies in Japan. Those who followed in Professor Kawasaki's footsteps were aided immeasurably by his efforts.

I will never forget one scholar, his eyes misting with open admiration as he observed: "An effort like that obviously deserves the Order of Cultural Merit. And to have done it without any official assistance—what an achievement!"

SELF-SUSTAINING STEREOTYPES

Professor Kawasaki compiled his dictionary as a way of promoting friendship between Japan and the Arab world; he also said that it was "a way of thanking the people in Arab countries who accorded me such great kindness and goodwill throughout my adult life."

In the classroom, he sought to open the eyes of his students as well: "Saying the word 'Arab' in Japan conjures a frightening image. But that's not the case at all. I assure you, you will never find a better friend. Arabs are sincere and hardworking. Because their culture is different from that of Japan or the West, some of you may feel a bit confused at first—but remember, if you think their behavior strange, they're thinking the same about you. It's mutual! The differences in customs and manners are really minor. We're all human; we laugh and cry over the course of our lives. Everyone wants to live in peace and enjoy life. We want our families to become happy. You know that originally 'Islam' also means 'peace'…"

Ignorance is a fearful thing. If we don't make the effort to discover the truth, simplistic stereotypes begin to take on a life of their own.

Since the early years of the Meiji era (1868–1912), the Japanese have studied Western civilization. Because we have been exposed to the glories of these cultures, we generally do not think of Europe as giving birth to Hitler, as a breeding ground for Nazism or as a particularly violent place. Nor do we view Christianity, which provides the West with its spiritual foundation, as dangerous.

In comparison, the Japanese people have scant knowledge of the Arab world. When an act of terror has been committed by people who happen to be Arabs, there is a rush to conclude that all Arabs are dangerous and that the Islamic faith encourages violence. Yet it is absurd to imagine that all 1.2 billion Muslims in the world are violent. Nor is the revival of Islam, often referred to as "Islamic fundamentalism," a monolithic mass movement. Within this diverse movement, the extremists are a small minority; the great majority are moderate.

Terrorism is of course contrary to the very spirit of religion, and the teachings of Islam do not in themselves foster terrorist acts.

Dr. Majid Tehranian, an Iranian national, is director of the Toda Institute for Global Peace and Policy Research, which I founded. As he explains it, the word *jihad* has at times been interpreted as "holy war" in Islam. In the strictest sense, however, the *jihad* that relies on armed force is external and minor. The "internal" *jihad* is understood to be the process of spiritual purification through which the evil that resides within, such as greed and hatred, is overcome. It is the latter that is deemed to be the "Great Jihad." Moreover, Islam teaches that the use of force may be permitted only in self-defense.

Incidentally, Japan also described World War II as a "holy war" even as it subjected the United States and the countries of Asia to repeated, violent assaults. The ideology of State Shinto was used to justify the war and stiffen national resolve. Yet if it were said that the Japanese and their culture are inherently violent, most people in Japan would surely contest such an assertion.

In any event, it would be dangerously naive to view the problems of the Middle East, entangled as they are with the Israeli–Palestinian conflict, the Gulf War and the interests of the oil and weapons industries, as a simple conflict between the "good guys" and the "bad guys."

Humankind will never see the light of peace as long as one party seeks to subjugate the other by force, with both sides caught in a vicious cycle of reprisals.

Torao Kawasaki first traveled to Egypt in 1935, dispatched by the Foreign Ministry as an exchange student. At the time, he was only 21, but this exceptional assignment was fully justified by his extremely assiduous approach to his studies.

He was born in 1914 in Hitachi, a port in Ibaraki Prefecture. His father was the leader of a band of fishermen. When he was growing up, the adults around him actively discouraged him from studying, saying that learning was of no use to a fisherman. Yet he somehow managed to get enrolled in what was then known as a middle school. A business venture started by his father failed, and household finances hit rock bottom. To make ends meet the family took on farming work in addition to fishing. The young Torao helped out, at times pushing a big-wheeled farm wagon. Every night, he rubbed his sleepy eyes as he continued his studies.

Eventually, he was admitted to Nagoya Commercial High School—now Nagoya University. He kept his promise never to be a burden to his family by excelling in school, which exempted him from paying tuition. He continued to study with ever increasing intensity, and the Foreign Ministry recruited him during his senior year. Upon joining the ministry, he was sent to Egypt to study.

It Also Snows in Arabia

In those days, the Japanese understanding of what was then known as Arabia amounted to little more than a place "somewhere beyond India." People had but a vague image of sand and camels, The Arabian Nights, Persian carpets and pyramids. Beyond that, they knew little—a state of ignorance that to a considerable degree persists to this day.

Professor Kawasaki often lamented how uninformed the Japanese were of the Arab world. "There are winters there, too. It even snows," he would say. "It may be called a desert, but there's more soil than sand... Islam is not a religion of the desert. On the contrary, it arose in the cities, through which people from many cultures passed. Coffee, sugar, alcohol, alkali, syrup, muslin, guitar, sofa—all these words have Arabic origins. And if you think about it, they all are accoutrements of civilized societies."

After graduating from Cairo University with a major in the Arabic language, he worked for the Japanese missions to Egypt, Lebanon and Iraq. It was a time when a number of Arab countries, which had been under

European colonial rule, were beginning to emerge from that humiliating experience and were struggling with the task of nation-building.

During the colonial era, the imperious attitude of their European rulers chafed Arabs, as if they were proclaiming that their political victory was a result of Christian superiority over Islam. It must have felt as though the Europeans were boasting, "If you want to modernize, you must forsake your backward Arab culture."

A proud people, the Arabs rejected this cultural domination even as they struggled with the daunting challenge of modernizing their societies and keeping their unique traditions alive. Professor Kawasaki felt great empathy for them, caught as they were between tradition and modernization. It was, after all, a dilemma that confronted Japan as well.

In the headlong rush to modernize, the Japanese had forsaken many worthwhile traditions, including their reverence for nature. Indeed, the Japanese today still suffer from the ill effects of the wholesale intake of Western culture, which has yet to be properly digested. Likewise, the tendency toward xenophobic nationalism in reaction to this "undigested" Westernization is a symptom common to Japan and the Arab countries.

IN THE WAKE OF WAR

Kawasaki returned to Japan after war broke out in the Pacific and, in 1944, he was sent to Indonesia, where Japanese defeat appeared imminent. He went as a naval administrator, a civilian post. He stayed on in Indonesia after the war's end to defend Japanese soldiers accused of war crimes in trials conducted by the Dutch, Indonesia's former colonial rulers.

Kawasaki faced a fierce dilemma. Clearly, the Japanese invasion had been wrong and there was no defending it. However, could a trial in which the victors judged the vanquished truly be fair? For almost all Japanese soldiers, there had been no choice but to obey the orders of the government and their superior officers.

Further, random chance seemed to play a big role in determining who would be branded a war criminal and who could return home. Soldiers were lined up, and if a local citizen picked one of them out, his fate was settled. Mistaken identity was a distinct possibility.

There were times when an interrogator would hit a suspect so violently that the sound would reverberate throughout the building. Worse still, trials were conducted without the presence of defense counsel.

The "fatherland" by whose order these men had gone to war not only failed to dispatch attorneys for their defense, it neglected to send any of the materials Kawasaki and his legal team so desperately required. Kawasaki and the 12 others who volunteered did everything they could to defend the accused. Despite their efforts, some of the men were convicted and sentenced to death.

On one occasion, Kawasaki had to attend the execution of a Japanese lieutenant by a firing squad, and he put down on paper what he saw. "Three patches of blood stained the pole to which the prisoner had been tied," he wrote after the lieutenant's body was carried away, covered in fresh blood. "I was reminded of the poppies that bloom in the fields of Iran and Central Asia…"

A PLEA FOR DIALOGUE

For how many millennia have blazing red poppies huddled together upon the continental expanses of Asia, bearing witness to wars and peace, the flourishing and fall of empires?

The dreams of heroes, princesses dressed in regal splendor, the joys and sorrows of everyday lives, the clash of arms and dust clouds whipped up by thundering hooves of cavalry… When all had been swept away like the passing of a great storm, only the flowers remained, blooming as if in remembrance of the wind.

When flowers can blossom innocently and without a thought, why must we humans repeat endless cycles of folly? Professor Kawasaki, with his large, jet-black eyes, must have peered at that time into the abyss of human history, the bottomless pit of our darker destiny.

On August 16, 1977, Professor Torao Kawasaki passed quietly away at the age of 63. His students bade him a fond and tearful farewell.

Some 15 years later, in 1992, I had the opportunity to visit Egypt and meet with Egyptian President Muhammad Hosni Mubarak to discuss the issue of peace in the Middle East. The president, who had worked to mediate between Israelis and the Arab countries, repeatedly emphasized that the region's future peace hinged on the success of persistent efforts toward dialogue. It was no longer possible, he said, to resolve these issues by force.

I agree that we must reach out to others through dialogue, repeatedly and regardless of the challenges involved. If we do not change the thinking that so easily turns to the use of force to settle disputes, the 21st century will become yet another century of war.

After meeting with the president, I left for the desert, where I thought back on the life of Professor Kawasaki and offered prayers for his repose. I informed his family of this and presented some photographs I had taken of the Pyramids.

Professor Kawasaki devoted his life to friendship with the Arab world and its people. He was a truly selfless man who did everything he could for the sake of peace.

I understand that "thank you" in Arabic is *shukran*. As the professor often noted, Arabic is indeed beautiful to the ear.

Looking up at the stars that burned brightly over Cairo, I softly called out to him. "Professor Kawasaki, *shukran*. *Shukran*, Professor Kawasaki."

BA JIN

Warrior of the Pen

BA JIN (1904–), PEOPLE'S REPUBLIC OF CHINA

Ba Jin is considered to be one of the most important and widely-read Chinese writers of the 20th century. During the Sino-Japanese war, he spoke out forcefully against the Japanese occupation. He was also critical of China's centuries-old feudalistic ethics. At the time of the Cultural Revolution he was persecuted as a counter-revolutionary but was later elected to many important national literary posts. His best-known works include the trilogy Family, Spring *and* Autumn.

Ba Jin

Warrior of the Pen

—❧—

"Youth is the hope of mankind." The renowned Chinese writer Ba Jin repeated this phrase several times over the course of our first meeting in 1980. Perhaps it is only natural that someone who has experienced severe persecution for his beliefs will come to trust only young people.

Though he was a respected writer who had called out for liberation from China's feudalistic traditions and encouraged the young to seek their own freedom, during the decade of China's Cultural Revolution (1966 1976)[2] Ba Jin was beaten and harassed. Like others considered a harmful influence, he was labeled "a great poisonous weed" and his writings were condemned as seditious. Now he has dedicated his life to leaving a record of his beliefs for the sake of future generations.

After hearing about the horrors he experienced, I could sense the profound weight of his statement about youth. In the same way, my beloved teacher, the second Soka Gakkai president Josei Toda, often stated with some bitterness: "I don't expect much from the old. I place my hopes in the young." He never forgot the memory of one friend after another

---

[2] Mass mobilization of urban Chinese youth under Mao Zedong which criticized Party officials, intellectuals and bourgeois values; many people died in the ensuing purges.

recanting their Buddhist faith in the face of imprisonment by the Japanese military authorities during World War II.

When fanaticism joins hands with authoritarian power, there is no limit to the cruelty human beings can inflict upon each other. What is it, I wonder, that lowers people to the level of wild animals?

REJECTING DEATH

Altogether, Ba Jin and I have met four times. Each time, I sensed behind his humility an inner strength that comes from unshakable conviction. Ruthless persecution drove many people to commit suicide during the Cultural Revolution; I once asked him if he had ever contemplated death during those bitter days. "No, I never considered it… I experienced much pain and hardship during that time, but through it all my only thought was, 'I have to keep fighting, I have to make it through to the very end.'"

During the Cultural Revolution, Ba Jin was treated in an utterly dehumanizing fashion. He was vilified as a "reactionary" and a "Mafia boss of the literary world." His house was raided by the Red Guards and his wife brutally beaten. Labeled a "monster and a demon," a hated class enemy, he was confined in one of many private prisons—nicknamed "the cowshed"—where he was tortured and interrogated for days on end. He was insulted, abused and denounced before a large public assembly, forced to confess to crimes he did not commit.

He was isolated from his friends and forbidden to write. His wife, his only support, was hounded to her grave. When she fell ill, she was refused treatment on the grounds that she was the wife of a "poisonous weed." By the time she was finally admitted to a hospital, it was already too late. She died three weeks later.

Even a decade after the Cultural Revolution, Ba spoke of being tormented by nightmares and emotional and mental scars so severe that he continued to experience them as actual physical pain.

At the beginning of the Cultural Revolution, Ba had believed the rhetoric of lofty goals and principles, but he soon realized that it was all a lie.

The Cultural Revolution, he realized, was little more than a chance for the Gang of Four and other self-declared "true soldiers of Revolution" to advance their own careers, which they did by stepping over the corpses of the innocent victims whom they framed and condemned to death for crimes that were never committed.

Ba Jin has written that the large number of cruel and inhuman acts that marked the Cultural Revolution were engendered by "a religious fanaticism cloaked in the robes of the Left."

He was robbed of everything, including his beloved wife and his work as a writer. Every effort was made to undermine his dignity as a human being. Yet when things were at rock bottom, he cried out defiantly to fate: "I will show you that I can survive!"

REBUILDING, RECORDING

Eventually, the storm passed. Surveying the ravaged state of his life and of society, Ba pledged to set down in writing the truth of the cruel deceits of the Cultural Revolution—as a warning to future generations and to prevent any recurrence. And he resolved not to die until he had accomplished that goal. Most other writers who had survived this period were so beaten down by their experiences that they never wrote again. I will never forget the light that flashed in his eyes as he shared this determination with me. There are things that cannot be destroyed by violence. There is a spiritual flame that flares higher and stronger, the harsher the efforts to stamp it out.

As a warrior of the pen, Ba Jin is heir to the spirit of his teacher, the great Chinese writer Lu Xun. Writing of his youthful days studying under Lu Xun, Ba compares his teacher to a character who appears in a short story by the Russian author Maxim Gorky. This character, Danko, a legendary folk hero, tore out his own blazing heart and used it as a torch to light the way for the people. In the same way, says Ba Jin, "Lu Xun for several decades illuminated my path with the flames of his burning heart." The importance of remembering his mentor's noble spirit is deeply etched in his mind; to this day, he says, the memory gives him the courage to go on.

When Ba Jin, by then president of the Chinese Writers' Association, gave a lecture in Kyoto in 1980, he declared:

> I do not write to earn a living or to build a reputation. I write to battle enemies. Who are they? Every outdated traditional notion, every irrational system that stands in the way of social progress and human development, and every instance of cruelty in the face of love. These are my great enemies.

> My pen is alight and my body aflame. Until both burn down to ash, my love and my hate will remain here in the world.

WRITING AND POLITICS

Born in 1904, Ba Jin confesses that age and ill-health at times make his pen feel as heavy as lead. Yet he continued to write every day, even if only a few lines. There is a fire in his heart that must be vented, debts of the soul that must be settled.

Several weeks after our first meeting in Japan, I had another opportunity to meet him, this time in Shanghai. He came to the hotel where I was staying and we discussed the subject of politics and literature. "The two are inseparable," he declared. "But politics can never take the place of literature, for it is only literature that builds the human spirit."

In this respect, Ba's view is rooted in the traditional Chinese creed that literature is both an important national endeavor and an immortal personal quest. For him, literature is anything but a diversion. It requires an awareness that each word, each sentence you write could sign your death warrant.

Some schools of literature carefully shun any interest in politics; such writing never denounces the abuses of the powerful. By contrast, literature that is lovingly engaged with the lives of the people inevitably scrutinizes the workings of governments and political leaders.

"No great work of literature has ever been composed at the command of a ruler," says Ba Jin. "It is always the people who determine literature's greatness." Writing, he asserts, is a matter of conveying truth and confronting lies.

In June 1984, I visited Ba Jin's home in Shanghai. "Our young writers are making such great strides that I almost can't keep up with them," he exclaimed. "I'm going to find myself left behind!" Delighting in the growth of the next generation and determined to continue progressing himself, Ba Jin's voice rang with the tones of eternal youth.

Concerned not to tire him, I took my leave early. He rose from his seat, determined to see me off. He picked up his walking stick and, supported by his daughter Li Xiaolin, walked with me out of the house and through the garden. Though I repeatedly asked him not to trouble himself any further, he insisted on walking with me through the gate, down the stone steps, all the way to the street. From the open car window, I saw a scene that remains to this day a treasured and indelible memory: Ba Jin and his entire family, including his grandchildren, smiling and waving at me.

Ba Jin once said: "Young people should always fight their own battles and make what they win their own. That is what it means to be young!"

LINUS PAULING

A Genius for Peace

LINUS PAULING (1901–94), UNITED STATES

Linus Pauling is the only person to have won two unshared Nobel Prizes—for chemistry in 1954 and for peace in 1962. As a young, insatiably curious scientist, he worked at the newly founded California Institute of Technology, home to the brightest minds of his time. His book The Nature of the Chemical Bond *(1939) is still a classic, and he is also considered the founding father of molecular biology. With his wife Ava Helen, he was a tireless campaigner for disarmament and for the halting of nuclear testing, authoring* No More War *in 1958.*

LINUS PAULING

A Genius for Peace

———

O n one occasion Dr. Pauling told me that he had continued to work for the peace movement because of his wife, Ava Helen. "I felt compelled," he said, "to earn and keep her respect." In that simple statement, I heard Dr. Pauling's heart. He wanted to do the right thing as a human being. That was what he had always fought for. He wanted his wife, the person who knew him best, to respect him. As long as he had that, he was afraid of nothing.

"Are you or are you not a communist?" This was the question that would be put to him at a state senate committee hearing that he had been summoned to appear before. In the 1950s, McCarthyism swept across the United States—a storm of anticommunist hysteria and witch-hunts. Dr. Pauling, as a proponent of world peace, opposed the U.S. government position on the necessity of nuclear weapons, and the authorities used subpoenas to appear before senate committees as a means of intimidation.

Of course, Dr. Pauling was not and never had been a communist. He was a humanist and a peace activist. "The enemy," he said, "is neither the Soviet Union nor America. The greatest enemy is war itself." True as this may be, it was a view that garnered very little support in those days. Dr. Pauling refused to state under oath that he was not a communist, because he didn't believe the government had a right to interfere in an individual's private beliefs. But if he continued to refuse, he would be cited for contempt.

How did Dr. Pauling deal with this dilemma? Immediately before he was to appear before the committee for a second time, he held a news conference where he declared to the gathered reporters that he was not a communist. Since he had already publicly announced his position, it would be absurd for the committee to ask him if he were communist. Nor could they cite him for contempt.

But the persecution continued, taking new and different forms. It extended even to his family. When it was announced that he had won the Nobel Prize in Chemistry in 1954, the authorities at first refused to issue the passport he needed to attend the award ceremony with his wife. He was subpoenaed and threatened time and again. He was also pressured by his university and forced to resign from his post.

A GREATER POWER

The age of madness eventually passed, however, and when it was gone, Dr. Pauling's reputation as a man of outstanding achievement and integrity remained. When he accepted the Nobel Peace Prize in 1962, he said: "I believe that there is a greater power in the world than the evil power of military force, of nuclear bombs—there is the power of good, of morality, of humanitarianism. I believe in the power of the human spirit."

He and Ava Helen continued to speak out. In the same year, 1962, they participated in a demonstration against nuclear weapons in front of the White House. When the demonstration was over, they changed into formal dress to attend a banquet for Nobel Laureates hosted by the president and first lady. The Kennedys were of course fully aware of the Paulings' activities earlier that day, and the president is said to have expressed his hope that they would continue to speak out on the issue.

Dr. Pauling is known as the father of modern chemistry. The British journal *New Scientist* called him one of the 20 greatest scientists of all time alongside Newton, Darwin and Einstein. He is the only person in history to have received two unshared Nobel Prizes.

I first met Dr. Pauling in February 1987. Though he would soon be 86 years old, he had come all the way to our newly opened Calabasas campus of Soka University of America in California so we could meet. Rain had fallen earlier, but the sky was clear when he arrived. The fresh greenery sparkled like gems. Dr. Pauling had traveled some 500 miles by plane and car from his home to get there. "I'm happy to cooperate in any way that I can for the sake of world peace," he said.

Though he was a great scholar and scientist, he was completely unaffected. In fact, he listened eagerly to what I had to say, even though I was young enough to be his son. He was a person of immense and embracing character. I met him four times, and each of those occasions is engraved in my memory like a scene from a film. I am very proud that we were able to see the publication of our dialogue, *A Lifelong Quest for Peace*, before he passed away.

YOUTHFUL STRUGGLES

How did Dr. Pauling become the genius that he was? Was he a child of privileged circumstances?

Dr. Pauling was born in 1901, the first year of the new century. His father died when he was nine. As a boy he was sickly, as was his mother. He had two younger sisters. He had no choice but to go to work, yet he also wanted to study. He attended high school but because of an error in school records, he never received his diploma.

Although he gained admission to university, he was so poor that he didn't even have enough money for regular meals. He had a donut for breakfast, skipped lunch, and ate at a cheap diner in the evening. "I was always hungry," he recalls. He had many part-time jobs while in college, doing any work he could find—he chopped firewood, worked as a kitchen hand and cleaner, and he also worked as a road paving inspector for a construction company.

One day, his aunt passed through a train station near the university. He met her there and she gave him two dollars. "Those were the most important two dollars I had ever received," he recalled. Yet even in these straitened circumstances, he continued to send money home to his mother. No matter how trying or disadvantageous his situation was, he always remained optimistic.

What makes for genius? Is it curiosity? Concentration? Determination and perseverance? At one of our meetings, I jokingly asked Dr. Pauling if there was some medicine that could make us smarter. He thought about it a moment, and then he said: "The only way is effort and more effort, really putting our minds to work until it hurts. And when it comes to children, we must give them the self-confidence that they can do anything if they try hard enough."

COMPASSIONATE ACTION

Dr. and Mrs. Pauling always took action to minimize the suffering of their fellow human beings. During World War II, they sheltered a Japanese-American in their home and were criticized and attacked for their stand. As soon as they learned of the bombing of Hiroshima and Nagasaki, they threw themselves into the peace movement. "I am fighting," says Dr. Pauling, "for those who cannot fight as hard as I."

In 1993, I gave a speech at Claremont McKenna College in Los Angeles. Dr. Pauling, 91 at the time, served as commentator, and in his remarks he declared that acting in the compassionate spirit of what Buddhism refers to as a bodhisattva is the true duty of all human beings.

An episode that took place when Dr. Pauling first visited Japan in 1955 demonstrates his character. After finishing a lecture at a university, he was walking with some other professors to his next appointment when they came upon a gate that was locked. The gate was in a fence about five feet high. The other professors set out to make a detour, but Dr. Pauling used a trash can standing nearby as a stepladder and blithely hopped over the fence.

The others with him were shocked for a minute. Dr. Pauling, the main guest, had gone ahead, leaving them there. What could they do but follow suit and hop over after him? Dr. Pauling was always this kind of person, a person who leaps lightly over the artificial fences that humanity builds.

When he was told that he was a scientist and should not express political opinions, he countered that that was wrong. All human beings, he firmly believed, have a responsibility to participate in political debate. It is very important for people to exercise their power to keep political leaders on the correct path. People's movements are absolutely necessary, he concluded.

In our last talk in 1993, a little more than a year before he passed away, I suggested that we organize an exhibition on his life and achievements. Four years after his death, the "Linus Pauling and the Twentieth Century: Quest for Humanity" exhibition was finally realized in September 1998. The fruit of the full cooperation of the Pauling family, including Dr. Pauling's son, Dr. Linus Pauling, Jr., a world-renowned psychiatrist, this exhibition has been shown in cities around the world.

A junior high school student who visited the exhibition wrote, "I now know that there is no such thing as a good war." In this way, Dr. Pauling's passionate appeal continues to be transmitted to young people who will shoulder the future of our planet in the 21st century.

I can see his face now, with his rosy cheeks and his big smile, saying, "How happy I am! This is a triumph for me and Ava Helen!"

My Reminiscences

Hearts Still Closed to the World?

HEARTS STILL CLOSED TO THE WORLD?
For much of its history, Japan remained a homogenous society cut off from the rest of the world. The author recalls his first encounters with foreigners in Japan and contemplates the fate of a nation that isolates itself behind a barrier of "difference."

MY REMINISCENCES

Hearts Still Closed to the World?

―✺―

When I was a boy, I loved going to the fairs held on Saturday nights. The main street leading to the east entrance of Kamata Railway Station, in what is now Ota Ward, Tokyo, would be lined with vendors' stalls and stands. In the summer, there were stalls for netting goldfish, stalls selling fireflies, water-balloon yo-yos and, later in the season, crickets trilling in ornate cages. There were stands for cotton candy, mint candy pipes, Chinese lantern plants, assorted hand-made sweets and baby chicks. The girls all flocked to the coloring book stands.

It was a time of few amusements, and strolling around the night fair offered children and adults alike an enjoyable time.

In the summer of 1937 I was nine years old. With a few coins that my mother had given me tightly clutched in my hand, I was wandering from stall to stall, looking at their offerings. The heat of the day had dissipated into the darkening sky, and it was becoming pleasant out. The street leading to the station was packed with a jostling crowd as people came out to walk in the cool evening air and take in the sights.

It was a peaceful scene—young and old, men and women, many wearing summer kimonos, making their way in the dim light cast by the lamps hanging in front of the stalls.

There was one stand at the end of a long row, belonging to a tall foreign vendor. He was thin and wore a gray suit. He was the first Westerner I had ever set eyes on.

"What is he selling?" I wondered. I wanted to go up and look, but at the same time I was afraid. In those days, unlike today, it was very rare to see a foreigner. I watched him from a short distance away.

He was selling Western-style razors. There were 50 or 60 lined up on his stand, and occasionally he would pick up two or three and call out cheerfully to the people walking past. I could hear him saying, in broken Japanese, "*Watashi, Nippon, daisuki desu* (I love Japan)."

For some reason, I found it hard to leave. I wondered if anyone would buy a razor. I stood there watching for some time, but people just walked by without stopping. He didn't make a single sale. It wasn't simply that his stand was in a poor location, either. The stands nearby were doing well enough.

The cold expressions on the faces of those who passed by seemed to say, "What? A down-and-out foreigner?" "What's he doing here?" People who had been talking and laughing looked startled and suddenly fell silent when they noticed him. Some even glared at him or showed their dislike with angry or disgusted expressions. The razor vendor couldn't have failed to notice all this, but he kept smiling and repeating, "*Watashi, Nippon, daisuki desu.*"

MYTH OF RACIAL SUPERIORITY

The attitudes of the passersby were probably influenced by the times. In February 1936 there had been an attempted coup in Tokyo, and then the Marco Polo Bridge Incident in July 1937 marked the beginning of all-out war between Japan and China.

At the time, the idea was drummed into the heads of Japanese citizens that their nation was an invincible "land of the gods" and they were superior to all other peoples. We children naturally came to believe that we were very fortunate to be born Japanese, and were glad that we hadn't been born in a foreign country. Our terrifyingly biased education etched racial prejudice into our impressionable young minds.

Of course, the purpose of propagandizing this supposed racial superiority was to justify Japan's invasion and domination of other Asian countries. The rest of the world, however, observed Japan's barbaric treatment of the peoples of Asia and were not about to believe Japan's fine-sounding claim of "liberating" Asia from Western imperialism.

Japan's educational system also taught the Japanese people a view of history and society acceptable only to people in their own country, which naturally led them to become estranged and then isolated from the perspectives of the international community.

False information is dangerous. So is concealing information.

In December 1937, Japanese military forces carried out what came to be known as the Rape of Nanking, but the facts went unreported to the people of Japan, who all cheered the glorious military victory and occupation of what was then the Chinese capital. Japanese war correspondents no doubt accompanied the invading forces, but none reported what actually happened. Nor did anyone report the outrage felt by the rest of the world.

We can't see our own backs, nor our own faces. For that we need a mirror. The leaders of Japan should have observed themselves in the mirror of their neighbors, the mirror of the world, the mirror of Asia. They should have humbly listened to the voices of their neighbors.

"AN ENEMY LANGUAGE"

I visited the night fair several times during the summer of 1937, and each time I couldn't resist checking on the tall foreigner's stall. It was always the same. He kept repeating "*Watashi, Nippon, daisuki desu*," and he never sold a single razor. Sometimes people gave him a hard time or made fun of him. He only responded to this harassment with a sad smile.

As I look back on the struggles of a foreigner running a stall at the night fair during an era like that, it's clear he really must've been in dire straits. I wondered then why everyone was so cold to him. Wasn't he a human being just like us? The way he was treated both angered and saddened me.

That summer was the last time I saw the razor vendor. As the war intensified, the lights of the night fairs gradually began to fade away.

Is a nation that rejects foreigners therefore kind to its own people? No, on the contrary—nationalism regards the nation or race as sacred, and sacrifices its citizens as a means for the nation's ends. In my family, my eldest brother was drafted in 1937 and, in the following year, two of my other older brothers were called into military service.

At about this time, essential foodstuffs such as rice, sugar, *miso* and soy sauce began to be rationed.

The ultranationalistic mood in Japan intensified as the years went by, and eventually English was banned as "an enemy language." At school, my friends talked about how from now on in baseball we would have to use Japanese words instead of the familiar "strike" and "ball" borrowed from English. Even the "HB" mark on pencils, indicating the hardness of the lead, was translated into Japanese, and the "Cherry" brand of cigarettes was renamed "Sakura," the Japanese word for that tree. Jazz and American movies were also banned. The syllables of the musical scale *do-re-mi-fa-sol-la-ti-do* were replaced in favor of the Japanese version, *ha-ni-ho-he-to-i-ro-ha*. And a pitcher for the Tokyo Giants baseball team, Victor Starffin, originally from Russia, was forced to take the Japanese name Hiroshi Suda.

In contrast to Japan, with its ever-narrowing inward focus, the American government at that time was conducting Japanese language training and research on Japan, in the belief that one needed to know one's opponent in order to win.

Recently in Japan, we are once again hearing with increasing frequency phrases that deliberately stress "ethnic pride" and "the superiority of Japanese culture." This may be a reaction to the loss of confidence accompanying the decline in the Japanese economy. Individuals, too, tend to put on a tough front when they lack self-confidence. They behave arrogantly because they have a strong sense of inferiority. But, even so, why do many

Japanese fixate on national and so-called racial heritage? Is it because they have not embraced the kind of universal values that transcend nation and race, such as human rights or those found in the great world religions?

DAWN AFTER AN AIR RAID

Just before the end of the war, some eight years after my encounter with the foreign razor vendor, I was looking up at the sky from a bomb shelter. I could see a squadron of B-29s illuminated by the searchlights. Their giant silver bodies glowed vermilion, reflecting the fires burning below. From the beginning of 1945, B-29 raids became a regular feature of our lives. The flames with which Japan had burned China and other countries of Asia and the South Pacific had returned to devour Japan.

Those who had a place to go in the countryside had already left Tokyo. The main street leading to Kamata Station was now filled with weather-beaten chests of drawers and other pieces of furniture left by people fleeing to the countryside. It was a sad sight. Any luggage too big to carry away had been abandoned along this street, as if it was a designated site for disposal. The pleasant night fairs were no more than a memory of a distant dream.

My hometown of Kamata had been engulfed in a great conflagration, cruel as hell itself, and was reduced to ashes. My family had to relocate from our home in Kojiya under government orders. We were to stay with an aunt in Magome, but just as we had finished moving, the house in Magome suffered a direct hit by an incendiary bomb during a major air raid on May 24. We had no choice but to live in a rough shack with a tin roof that we built on top of the burned-out site.

One night, the air-raid sirens were wailing, and the radio announced stridently: "A large squadron of B-29s has entered the Imperial capital." We rushed into our bomb shelter. My younger brothers and sister, my cousins and perhaps some neighbors were in there with me.

My four older brothers were all away at the war and my father was ill. At 17, I was forced to think of myself as the mainstay of our family. And so on that night I was looking out of the entrance of the dugout to see what was going on.

The shells from the Japanese antiaircraft guns, aimed at the B-29s, flew through the sky like fireworks. However, they rarely hit anything.

While in the end there was no direct attack on Magome, I nevertheless spent a sleepless night. Just around dawn, about a hundred B-29s flew away majestically, heading into the eastern horizon. Though they were the planes of the enemy, they were a magnificent sight, and I watched them until they were tiny dots in the distant sky.

Just then someone shouted, "Hey! What's that?" Something was falling from the sky. I took a close look. It was a parachute. A plane must have been hit and now an enemy airman was falling from the sky.

An "American Barbarian"

The parachute seemed to be coming right at me. I was startled. "He might shoot me!" I thought, but I couldn't move. I just stood there, watching the trajectory of the falling enemy. It was only a few moments, but it seemed like hours.

The American soldier dropped something. "Maybe it's important secret documents!" I wondered, but I couldn't take my eyes off him. The parachute continued to come straight at me. Then, with tremendous speed, it flew over my head. The whiteness of the skin of the soldier's arm sticking out of his short-sleeved shirt reminded me that he really was a "white man."

He passed by me so closely that I could see his face. I was astonished at how young he was, almost like a child. He was an innocent-looking blonde youth who might have been all of 20 years old.

He was completely different from the "barbaric Americans and British" that we had been taught to expect. This was a phrase frequently employed at the time, and when American soldiers or U.S. and British leaders were depicted in magazines, they were shown as monstrous, savage brutes. The gap between the reality of the young man who had passed not far from me and the images that had been pounded into us was too great, and I was confused. Could this be one of those vicious enemy soldiers? Was this a soldier of the American military which, in day after day of indiscriminate bombing, had been responsible for burning and killing my friends and defenseless young children?

The parachuting airman landed in a field some 200 or 300 meters away. I was relieved that the danger was over. Somewhere along the way, I noticed that any feelings of hostility I'd had toward him had completely vanished.

After a brief rest, at around 7:00 a.m. I went outside again. I was concerned about the object that the American had dropped. It was a quiet morning, and it seemed as if the air raid of the night before had been only a dream. I looked around for a while, and then I found the object. It was a thick package wrapped in white bandages. I delivered it to the neighborhood police station, and the elderly policeman immediately telephoned someone and made a report. He seemed agitated, tense.

I left the station. As I was walking along, wondering what had become of the young American soldier, I came upon a circle of people talking on the side of the street. They were discussing him.

Apparently, as soon as he landed, a group of people ran up to him and began beating him with sticks. Someone also dashed up with a Japanese sword, threatening to kill him. Beaten nearly senseless, he was eventually led away by the military police, his arms tied behind his back and his eyes blindfolded.

Hearing this, I felt tremendous pity for him. Surely, he hadn't come to fight this war out of any desire to do so, I thought.

When I got back and told my mother what had happened, she said, "How awful! His mother must be so worried about him."

After the war, I learned that a considerable number of American airmen were shot down over Japan. Sometimes they were treated kindly by the Japanese, but in many cases, though already injured, they were beaten or killed. I had heard of an incident where a person armed with a bamboo spear lunged at a captive soldier, shouting: "The Americans killed my son! Let me take a stab at him!" Anyone who dared call for restraint in such a scene ran the risk of being accused of treason: "So you're sympathizing with the enemy? Are you Japanese?!" This was the atmosphere in Japan at the time. If one tried to be a human being, one was accused of being a traitor to the nation, and if one wanted to be a patriot, one could not avoid being a traitor to humanity. Even the simple human act of sympathizing with another was forbidden.

My encounters with the foreign razor vendor and the downed young American soldier—taking place at the beginning of Japan's war with China and at the end of World War II—were both sad events. I do not know what became of either man.

More than half a century has passed since then, and now the majority of Japanese have never experienced war. The postwar generation does not bear responsibility for causing the war, but they do have a responsibility to oppose the ultranationalistic tendencies and intolerant ideas existing in Japan today that can lead to war. To fail to oppose them, to fail to act, to remain silent is a passive form of support for such ideas.

A foreign resident of Japan has said: "It's because I love Japan that I want it to be a country trusted by the world and respected by its neighbors. If it goes on as it is, ignoring human rights, ignoring the facts of history, shutting its ears to the concerns of its neighbors, it will be ridiculed and disregarded by all. I speak out because I am so terribly worried that this might happen."

From a distant memory, I hear the voice of the man in the faded gray suit calling out: "*Watashi, Nippon, daisuki desu.*"

⟿

OSVALDO PUGLIESE

The Passion of the Tango

OSVALDO PUGLIESE (1905–95), ARGENTINA

Pugliese received his first music lessons from his father, a shoemaker and amateur flutist, and went on to become a giant of the tango. His uncompromising musicality and frequent innovations as a pianist, composer and arranger left an indelible mark on the history of the tango and continue to influence its development. He was frequently blacklisted and even jailed for his political beliefs, his music sometimes banned from being broadcast. None of this succeeded in diminishing his popularity.

OSVALDO PUGLIESE

The Passion of the Tango

—◦—

I admire people who are completely devoted to their chosen vocation. The Argentine pianist and composer Osvaldo Pugliese was such a person; he was tango incarnate. He once said: "My fingers are as hard as nails. I'm just a carpenter, hammering away at the piano keys." His life was inextricably interwoven with the century-old history of tango.

When we met shortly before his death, I asked him how he would define tango. Pugliese responded, "It is the folk music of the Argentine people, born from their hearts. It first emerged in the lower class districts near Buenos Aires, and for a time it was regarded as indecent and disreputable. But the people took it into their hearts, and there it put down deep roots. Today, it is our national music and is loved by people all over the world."

Tango has been elevated into an international art form, and Pugliese played a major role in this. After World War II, tango enjoyed a boom in Japan, and in Tokyo alone there were dozens of "tango coffee shops."

Tango is filled with poetry, pathos, longing for freedom and prayers of hope. It expresses the laughter of a young maiden, the whispered murmurs of her suitors, their yearning for love and the warmth of its fulfillment. Tango is wild but sophisticated, humorous and raging. It is stylish, beautiful and fierce. Its rhythms pulsate with an inexpressible melancholy, a mournful yearning that cannot be expressed in words.

POWERFUL EMOTIONS

The famous tango rhythm that reaches into the very core of one's being pulsed vibrantly in Pugliese's veins. He was born in downtown Buenos Aires in 1905, among factories and low-rent apartment buildings where workers stricken with tuberculosis and poor immigrant families lived packed together in close proximity. But the people were warm and affectionate, and gave free and unrestrained expression to the full gamut of human emotion—joy, anger, aspiration, disappointment and sorrow.

His father, Adolfo, worked in the shoe industry, but also played the flute in a tango band. "My father took me everywhere with him," he recalled, "exposing me to the diversity of the world of tango."

Pugliese's serious, scholarly demeanor disguised a soul seething with powerful emotions. "We are sailing on the vast ocean of tango," he once told the members of his orchestra: "The important thing is to know the currents that will lead us to the harbor of the people's hearts. Tango must always be interpreted in terms of human emotions. It has a human voice."

This offers us a glimpse into the secret of Pugliese's long musical career. He always asked himself, "What do people really want? What are they feeling in the depths of their hearts?" As a tango player, you need to keep your ears tuned to the times, listening until you can physically sense what people are feeling. You need to constantly strive for self-renewal until you yourself become an instrument that plays in harmony with the voices of the people.

"We can't do the same thing we were doing ten years ago. We must always find something new; we must always be thinking about tomorrow," said Pugliese, who included a new composition even in his final concert tour before retiring from the stage in 1989 at the age of 84. His musical career spanned seven decades, and his music won the hearts of four generations. The reasons for his success were his iron determination to always stay in tune with the people and his faith in their infinite creativity. "The people have always been my greatest teacher," he declared.

It is a mistake to divide artistic genres into elevated and vulgar arts. There are vulgar artists in the classical tradition, and extremely sophisticated and accomplished artists working in popular genres. Pugliese himself began by studying classical music. "My mother always encouraged my efforts," he recalled. "When I was practicing the piano, she would often stand by the door watching me warmly." One day, she made the chance remark that it would be wonderful if he could perform some day at the Teatro Colón, which is one of the three great opera houses of the world and a monument to classical music, where only the finest artists are invited to perform. "For us, poor as we were, to perform at the Teatro Colón seemed an impossible dream."

To support himself and his family, he switched from classical music to tango, and from the age of 15 began earning his living as a professional musician. He started, he said, by playing the musical accompaniment to silent movies in theaters. He recalled: "In those days, I would earn four pesos for playing all night in a cafe. The next morning I always gave my earnings to my mother."

After a long apprenticeship, he finally formed a band of his own in 1939, when he was 33. He and the other band members worked persistently—stubbornly—to create their own sound, and were finally rewarded with explosive popularity. This was at a time when popular orchestras that had merely contented themselves with following the trends of the day were disbanding one after another.

EXACTING STANDARDS

Pugliese was incredibly demanding. When you joined his orchestra, colleagues would say, your whole life was spent rehearsing and performing. He once spent three days rehearsing two bars of music until he was completely satisfied. He was always the first to arrive at the auditorium, and the

first to begin rehearsing. His perfect technique and enthusiastic perform-
ances established his position at the pinnacle of the world of the tango.

He was always devoted to learning. He studied and taught himself
music theory with exacting thoroughness and dedication.

His will was simply unbreakable. He was imprisoned several times,
accused of communist sympathies, but he always remained unbowed. In
1968, he faced a crisis when the members of his orchestra, which he had
nurtured warmly for so many years, left him to establish a new group just
before the orchestra's 30th anniversary. Everyone thought that his career
had come to an end. But he did not let this setback deter him. Within six
months, he launched a new orchestra. Everyone applauded the undaunted
determination of the venerable maestro.

In 1985, an unforgettable event in the history of tango took place:
Pugliese was invited to perform a recital at the Teatro Colón. Before the
start of the performance, a poet introduced him to the audience with the
following words:

> *A man of pure, uncompromising melody,*
> *A man of the slums and the skyscrapers,*
> *A man who wrote many of his compositions behind*
> *bars and under the cold gaze of surveillance,*
> *A man who brought the dawn with his songs that*
> *resound through our streets.*
>
> . . . .
>
> *Now Pugliese will sit down at this piano*
> *At our request.*

The applause was thunderous as he greeted the audience. He had only
one thing to say at this glorious moment. "To my mother, who loved music
more than anything, this Teatro Colón was heaven." He sat down and
began to play. The dream that began 65 years before had finally come true.
It was a brilliant triumph, the victory of a man who had made his life
among the people.

Pugliese was not egotistical. Though he was made an honorary citizen of Buenos Aires and, along with many other honors, received the French Government's prestigious Culture Award, what really made him happy was that the once-scorned tango had finally received the recognition it deserved.

He was also well known for instituting a policy for the payment of his orchestra members, including himself, whereby all shared fairly in the earnings. And after his retirement, he sold his personal possessions to create a "House of Tango," dedicated to preserving the history and tradition of Argentinian tango, teaching and fostering a new generation of musicians and performers to ensure its future.

When I visited Buenos Aires in 1993, not only did Mr. Pugliese come with his wife, Lidia, to greet me at the airport, but he agreed to perform at a cultural festival organized by Soka Gakkai International members in Argentina. This in itself was something of a news event in Argentina, but people were even more astonished when he brought his entire orchestra to rehearse at the venue two days before the festival.

"I don't like to sit at home," he once said. "I want to be out among people, creating something together with them." His action was in perfect accord with this credo. When his piano was delivered, the then 87-year-old Pugliese showed his amazing youthfulness by trying to push it into place himself!

On the day of the festival, he played the piece he had written for me as a token of our friendship, *"Tokio Luminoso"* or "Shining Tokyo." As we applauded his vigorous performance, I recalled what he had said to me in Japan: "I want to work with you for peace, so that we do not repeat the tragedies of the past. I will fight. To the very end, to the moment of my death, I will fight for human victory." And he was true to his word.

Hazel Henderson

A Message of Hope

HAZEL HENDERSON (1933–), UNITED STATES

Hazel Henderson is a futurist, evolutionary economist and consult-ant on sustainable development who has written eight books includ-ing Building a Win-Win World: Life Beyond Global Economic Warfare. *Her first step into environmental activism was as founder of the group "Citizens for Clean Air" in New York in 1964. She serves on the boards of the Calvert Group which promotes ethical investment, the New Economics Foundation and the Club of Budapest.*

HAZEL HENDERSON

A Message of Hope

⟶⟵

D r. Hazel Henderson describes her wide-ranging activities—she is an environmentalist, an author and an economist—as those of a "futurist." She also insists that her ideal is to be a whole human being. I find her approach deeply inspiring. Only humans envisage a better, more valuable future and make efforts toward its realization. To believe in the future is to believe in humanity. A futurist is engaged in the scholarship of hope.

Traditional economics is based on a very pessimistic view of human nature; it is assumed that people are essentially selfish, that our actions are motivated solely by the urge to maximize profit. But, Dr. Henderson questions, what about all the things people do without any thought of gain, the acts of "caring and sharing" that she has witnessed time and again? Traditional economics focuses only on competitive activities in which currency is exchanged. But what about spontaneous acts of collaboration and cooperation, the work of volunteers and citizens groups, for example, that enhance the quality of life for people? What about the gifts of nature itself? What about the energy generated by the sun, without whose warmth and light, life on Earth would be unthinkable? Shouldn't these also be accorded value?

Such questions have pushed Dr. Henderson toward a radical rethinking of economic theory, one aspect of which she calls the "love economy"—all those things people do, not in quest of profit, but simply out of love. The United Nations has estimated the value of such unpaid labor at US $16 trillion annually—11 trillion by women, 5 trillion by men. By taking all of these factors into account, Dr. Henderson has developed a view of economic activity that is actually far more "realistic" than that of traditional economists.

Measuring Soot

It was concern for the future that inspired an "ordinary housewife" (her own words) to engage in the intensive self-study of economics that has enabled her to successfully challenge the views of Nobel laureates.

Living in New York City in the 1960s, Hazel founded the group Citizens for Clean Air because, as she says, "We were anxious that our children have the best future possible. Thinking back, I realize that's what gave us the strength to endure numerous persecutions and keep pushing ahead."

It all started when she noticed that her daughter was coming home stained with soot that even the most vigorous scrubbing wouldn't remove. She herself was suffering from a persistent cough. Something wasn't right. She started talking to the other mothers at the neighborhood park as they watched their children playing. Starting with the simple question, "Don't you think the air here is bad?" she engaged the mothers in discussions that eventually led to the formation of Citizens for Clean Air.

Dr. Henderson began using the time during her daughter's afternoon naps to write letters to the mayor and other city officials. Eventually, she received a reply from the mayor stating that what she thought was pollution was probably just mist rolling in from the sea. Not discouraged by this irresponsible reply, she investigated further and found the city actually kept measurements of soot particles in the city's air on a daily basis.

She and her group, which now had about ten members, started urging the TV networks to include air pollution data in the daily weather forecasts. Dr. Henderson wrote to the chairman of the Federal Communications Commission (FCC) in Washington, DC, responsible for assuring that broadcasts were consistent with "the public interest, convenience, and necessity." Using common sense and a natural understanding of human nature, she wrote to all the major TV networks, enclosing photocopies of encouraging letters she had received from the chairman of the FCC and New York Governor Nelson Rockefeller. A few weeks later, she was surprised to receive a phone call from the vice-president of one of the major New York television stations. A month later, the New York Air Pollution Index was on the air. Three months later, all TV stations, most radio stations, and local newspapers were covering the index.

Encouraged by this success—the outcome of the courage that refused to give up—Dr. Henderson started taking on new challenges, one after another. "I felt I ought to say out loud what I had to say. Nobody could stop me." Many people assume that it is impossible to achieve change. They think the obstacles are too vast. But Hazel was confident that a way could be found if people who shared the same concerns joined forces. She had assumed that there would be difficulties and admits that she finds them exciting.

TO WHAT END ECONOMICS?

Born in England in 1933, Dr. Henderson never received formal university training in economics. At age 16 she began working at a local women's clothing shop and later in a hotel. She comments that she studied in the university of human life. There she learned that all people have potential, that even sales clerks—such as herself—have great untapped capacity.

When Hazel was 25 she moved to the United States and worked selling airline tickets. She married, and it was the simple desire to have her daughter breathe clean air that inspired her tireless efforts that continue to this day.

We first met in 1998 and since then have engaged in an energetic exchange of ideas and views. For me there are few pleasures that match that of interacting with someone who is working with all-out dedication to a cause, sustained by clear and deeply-held beliefs. In our first meeting she described the early years of effort waged largely alone. The response of politicians and experts to her appeals for cleaner air was always the same: It costs too much money; we can't do it. Lurking behind such responses she often sensed contempt: What does a housewife like you know about the way the world really works?

But she wasn't put off. If economic theories require that we destroy the environment and make people suffer, there must be something wrong with the theories. She began thinking about the kind of economics that would be focused on people's happiness. Her approach is simple, it could be called naïve, but that is her strength. If something doesn't seem right to the ordinary citizen, it probably isn't. The activities of professionals in all fields—be it politics, medicine, communications or religion—are for the sake of the people who lack specialized knowledge and skills. Arrogance takes hold and everything goes awry the moment such specialists start telling the "amateurs" to shut up and keep their opinions to themselves.

Feeling the need to arm herself with knowledge, she wrote to many colleges asking if they had courses on how ecology related to economics, biology, sociology, anthropology and physics. Her ideal has always been to view things in a holistic way. But there were no such courses available, so she began an extensive program of self-study in economics and other fields. When she found an author whose ideas inspired her, she would send off a letter; in this way she developed personal mentoring relationships with many leading thinkers, including Dr. Ernst Schumacher, author of *Small Is Beautiful*.

Dr. Henderson credits her parents with instilling an attitude of not blindly accepting what she was told. She learned to stop and think for herself before making judgments. As her research efforts progressed, she came to question more and more of the core assumptions of modern economics. How meaningful, for example, are statistics that include in the measure of economic growth activities that pollute the environment or harm people's health while ignoring the related costs?

Economics, she soon concluded, despite the complex and seemingly precise mathematical formulas in which it is expressed, is not a science at all. Rather than being a neutral, value-free science, she found that economics focuses on justifying the gains of the winners and silencing the losers. It is really politics in disguise. Her ideas horrified traditional economists. She was publicly insulted and dismissed. On one television program, an economist sitting next to her said, "She is a nice lady, but she doesn't know a thing about economics." She responded to such criticism by buying more books and studying even harder. Letters were sent to her husband's employer calling her a communist. "That was very hurtful," she says, "because it was the furthest thing from my mind." In one corporate public relations newsletter she even was referred to as "one of the most dangerous women in the United States"—a title she now wears with pride.

FINDING ONENESS

Her expertise and unique and forward-looking proposals eventually gained recognition. From 1974 to 1980 she served on the U.S. Congress Office of Technology Assessment Advisory Council. She has advised more than 30 governments on their economic policies. Her columns are carried in some 400 newspapers in 27 countries worldwide. She has helped promote the concept and practice of ethical investing, for those who wish to be sure that their investments support ecologically and socially sustainable corporate practices, and developed an index of indicators which measure quality of life much more effectively than the narrow scales which only consider so-called economic growth.

Among her close friends is Mikhail Gorbachev. In the fall of 1995, when there were rumors abroad that he was considering a return to political life, it was Dr. Henderson who advised him not to limit his concern to the affairs of a single country but to work for the good of the entire planet.

Throughout it all she has remained first and foremost a citizen activist, committed to building, through informing and educating people, grassroots solidarity for a better future. The title of one of her books sums up the essence of that vision: *Building a Win-Win World*. She wants, in other words, to help humanity move beyond a system that produces winners and losers.

Buddhism teaches that we live within a framework of interdependence—that we need one another and offer each other essential support in seen and unseen ways. The same relationship exists between humans and the natural environment. Without the freely-given blessings of nature we could not exist for even a moment. It is this sense of appreciation that leads Dr. Henderson to speak of "Mother Sun"—the nearest star that provides all the essential energy for our planet. Buddhism also teaches the ultimate unity of humankind—a belief in the universally human dimension that encompasses and transcends our difference and diversity.

From her own mother, Dr. Henderson absorbed a "tremendous faith that human beings, at their core, wherever they are on this planet and whatever their culture, can come to accept their oneness." When they traveled together, her mother was always able to overcome differences of culture and language: "She always achieved total human-level communication. For her, it was all body language. She would find other mothers, sit with them in parks, admire their babies: 'What a lovely baby, may I pick your baby up?'"

As we move into an economy that is less about building the "hardware" of factories and machines and more about software and services, Dr. Henderson expects that the special talents of women as harmonizers and communicators will come more into play. She believes that women have a special commitment to and aptitude for peace.

"Women," she says, "know how much time, love and effort goes into raising a child. When war arises, all that is reduced to nothing… this is why women's active participation in conflict resolution is of great importance." Having observed debates between high-level Israeli and Palestinian women, she states with confidence: "If those women had been empowered and fully represented in negotiations, there would have been a peace settlement decades ago."

During our talks, we spoke about the concept of human revolution. In the years after Japan's defeat, my mentor, Josei Toda, brought a message of hope to people who had borne the brunt of war and its aftermath. It was his assertion that a profound change in the life of a single individual could change the direction of an entire society. Dr. Henderson concurred with this: "We have the power to alter our destiny. This is very much my own view. This is what my work for the last 30 years has been all about."

FURTHER READING

ARNOLD TOYNBEE

Arlen, Michael J. *Passage to Ararat.* St. Paul, MN: Ruminator Books, 2002. New York: Farrar, Straus & Giroux, 1975. 1st edition.

Miller, Donald E. and Lorna Touryan Miller. *Armenia: Portraits of Survival and Hope.* Berkeley: University of California Press, 2003.

Toynbee, Arnold J. *The Western Question in Greece and Turkey: A Study in the Contact of Civilisations.* London: Constable and Company, Ltd., 1923.

———— and Daisaku Ikeda. *Choose Life: A Dialogue.* Ed. by Richard L. Gage. London: Oxford UP, 1975.

JOSE ABUEVA

Abueva, Jose. *The Making of the Filipino Nation and Republic.* Quezon City: University of the Philippines Press, 1998.

Setsuho, Ikehata and Ricardo Trota Jose, eds. *The Philippines under Japan: Occupation Policy and Reaction.* Quezon City: Ateneo de Manila University Press, 1999.

Yu-Jose, Lydia. *Japan Views the Philippines, 1900–44.* Manila: Ateneo de Manila University Press, 1992.

NELSON MANDELA

Coetzee, P. H. and A.P. J. Roux, eds. *The African Philosophy Reader.* London: Routledge, 1998.

Meer, Fatima. *Higher Than Hope: The Authorized Biography of Nelson Mandela.* New York: Harper & Row, Publishers, 1990.

Stubbs, Aelred, ed. *Steven Biko—I Write What I Like: A Selection of His Writings.* San Francisco: Harper & Row, Publishers, 1978.

VALENTINA TERESHKOVA
Tereshkova, Valentina and A. Lothian. *Valentina: First Woman in Space.* Edinburgh: The Pentland Press Limited, 1997.

MAHATMA GANDHI
Gandhi, M. K. *Gandhi on Non-Violence—A Selection from the Writings of Mahatma Gandhi.* Ed. by Thomas Merton. New York: New Directions Publishing Corporation, 1965.

Nehru, Jawaharlal. *The Discovery of India.* New Delhi: Jawaharlal Nehru Memorial Fund/Oxford UP, 1992.

Wolpert, Stanley. *Gandhi's Passion: The Life and Legacy of Mahatma Gandhi.* Oxford: Oxford UP, 2001.

DAISAKU IKEDA – WORLD WAR II JAPAN
Buruma, Ian. *Wages of Guilt: Memories of War in Germany and Japan.* London: Vintage/Random House, 1995.

Cries for Peace. Comp. by the Youth Division of Soka Gakkai. Tokyo: The Japan Times, Ltd., 1978.

Ienaga, Saburo. *The Pacific War: World War II and the Japanese, 1931–1945.* New York: Pantheon Books, 1978.

Shillony, Ben-Ami. *Politics and Culture in Wartime Japan.* Oxford: Clarendon Press, 1991.

CHINGIZ AITMATOV
Aitmatov, Chingiz. *The Day Lasts More Than a Hundred Years.* Trans. by John French. Bloomington: Indiana University Press, 1988.

RABBI MARVIN HIER
Hier, Rabbi Marvin, writer. *Echoes That Remain.* Documentary. Dir. Arnold Schwartzman. Simon Wiesenthal Center, 1990.

FANG ZHAOLING

Chinese Painting by Fang Zhaoling. University Museum and Art Gallery, HKU, 1988.

Fang Zhaoling. *Works by Fang Zhaoling.* Hong Kong UP 1992.

MARTIN SELIGMAN

Seligman, Martin. *Learned Optimism: How to Change Your Mind and Your Life.* New York: Pocket Books, 1998.

DAVID NORTON

Norton, David L. *Imagination, Understanding, and the Virtue of Liberality.* Lanham, MD: Rowman & Littlefield, 1996.

CORNELL CAPA

Capa, Cornell. *The Concerned Photographer.* New York: Grossman, 1968.

Capa, Robert. *Images of War.* London: Paul Hamlyn, 1964.

————. *Robert Capa Photographs.* New York: Aperture, 1996.

ROSA PARKS

Parks, Rosa. *Dear Mrs. Parks: A Dialogue with Today's Youth.* New York: Lee and Low Books, 1996.

———— . *My Story.* New York: Dial Books, 1992.

JAN ØBERG

Fischer, Dietrich, Wilhelm Nolte and Jan Øberg. *Winning Peace: Strategies and Ethics for a Nuclear-free World.* New York: Crane Russak, 1989.

Øberg, Jan. "Misguided motives led to the chaos in Kosovo." Opinion. Kosovo: Prospects for Peace. CNN. <http://www.cnn.com/SPECIALS/2000/kosovo/stories/present/kfor/>.

TORAO KAWASAKI
Kawasaki, Torao. *Sirukurodo no Arabu-jin* (Arabians on the Silk Road), Kyoto: Chugai-Nippo-Sha, 1996.

BA JIN
Ba Jin. *The Family.* Trans. by Sidney Shapiro. Peking: Foreign Languages Press, 1978.

Martin, Helmut and Jeffrey Kinkley, eds. *Modern Chinese Writers: Self-portrayals.* Armonk, NY: M.E. Sharpe, 1992.

LINUS PAULING
Marinacci, Barbara, ed. *Linus Pauling in His Own Words.* New York: Touchstone/Simon & Schuster, 1995.

———— and Ramesh Krishnamurthy, eds. *Linus Pauling on Peace: A Scientist Speaks Out on Humanism and World Survival.* Los Altos, CA: Rising Star Press, 1998.

Mead, Clifford and Thomas Hager, eds. *Linus Pauling: Scientist and Peacemaker.* Corvallis: Oregon State UP, 2001.

Pauling, Linus and Daisaku Ikeda. *A Lifelong Quest for Peace: A Dialogue.* Trans. and ed. by Richard L. Gage. Boston: Jones and Bartlett Publishers, 1992.

OSVALDO PUGLIESE
Lozza, Arturo Marcos. *Osvaldo Pugliese al Colón* (Osvaldo Pugliese at the [Teatro] Colón). Buenos Aires: Editorial Cartago, 1985.

HAZEL HENDERSON
Henderson, Hazel. *Building a Win-Win World: Life Beyond Global Economic Warfare.* San Francisco: Berrett-Koehler Publishers, 1996.

————. *Thinking Globally, Acting Locally: The Politics and Ethics of the Solar Age.* Lecture. Berkeley: University of California, 1982.

———— and Daisaku Ikeda. *Planetary Citizenship: Your Values, Beliefs and Actions Can Shape a Sustainable Future.* Santa Monica, CA: Middleway Press, 2004.

ABOUT THE AUTHOR

Daisaku Ikeda was born in Tokyo on January 2, 1928. He is a leading Buddhist philosopher and a prolific writer who has published over 100 works. As well as poetry, he writes on topics related to peace, education and the human condition.

Ikeda's life was fundamentally shaped by his youthful experience of World War II and his eldest brother's accounts of the atrocities committed by the Japanese military in China. The search for a means to root out the fundamental causes of human conflict thus became a driving force in his life from a young age.

After the war, Ikeda came to embrace Buddhism through his encounter with Josei Toda, leader of the Soka Gakkai lay Buddhist group. In 1960, he succeeded Toda as head of the Soka Gakkai and he has played a central role in the spread and development of Nichiren Buddhism outside Japan. He is currently president of Soka Gakkai International (SGI).

Ikeda has recently published a collection of poetry in English, *Fighting for Peace*, and many volumes in Japanese. He is founder of the Institute of Oriental Philosophy, the Boston Research Center for the 21st Century, the Toda Institute for Global Peace and Policy Research and the Soka education system.